A Pilgrim in Ireland

A Pilgrim in Ireland

✺ A Quest for Home ✺

Frances Greenslade

PENGUIN

VIKING

VIKING
Published by the Penguin Group
Penguin Books Canada Ltd, 10 Alcorn Avenue, Toronto, Ontario,
Canada M4V 3B2
Penguin Books Ltd, 80 Strand, London WC2R 0RL, England
Penguin Putnam Inc., 375 Hudson Street, New York,
New York 10014, U.S.A.
Penguin Books Australia Ltd, 250 Camberwell Road, Camberwell,
Victoria 3124, Australia
Penguin Books (NZ) Ltd, cnr Rosedale and Airborne Roads, Albany,
Auckland 1310, New Zealand

Penguin Books Ltd, Registered Offices: Harmondsworth, Middlesex,
England

First published 2002

1 3 5 7 9 10 8 6 4 2

Printed and bound in Canada on acid free paper ⊗

NATIONAL LIBRARY OF CANADA CATALOGUING IN PUBLICATION DATA

Greenslade, Frances, 1961–
A pilgrim in Ireland : a quest for home

ISBN 0-670-91112-7

1. Greenslade, Frances, 1961– . Journeys—Ireland.
2. Ireland—Description and travel. 3. Spirituality. I. Title.

DA978.2.G73 2002   914.1504'824   C2002-900187-0

Visit Penguin Canada's website at **www.penguin.ca**

To the memory of my mother, Veronica Kathleen Greenslade

1.
HOME

And again I awake to find myself packing to leave. . . .
Today the Okanagan sky is fresh with wind.
Tomorrow is where an old lady sits staring at a wall.
The end of this journey somewhere just beyond her.

—ARMAND GARNET RUFFO, "SHE ASKED ME"

ON A DYING-DOWN INDIAN SUMMER DAY, I turn off the highway and climb the winding road to the gathering. We're in a valley hemmed in by hills rimmed with silhouettes of feathered firs. Teepees and tents circle the grounds, and if not for the line of cars parked in the shade of the trees, there would be no reason to believe this community hasn't always been here.

I'm part of the neophyte vegetable-chopping crew led by John, a professional cook who rises to the challenge of making do in our makeshift kitchen. Pots clatter, laughter bubbles like soup, and across the field comes drumming, low and steady like a heartbeat. Burning maple pops and hisses, and the woodstove kicks. A blue flame flickers on the propane stove. In the half-light of falling dusk, Alex, with lawnchair wings folded under each arm, improvises a joyful eagle dance across the wet grass. Tonight there'll be seven of us in a teepee, stretched out in our blankets, edging closer to the fire as the night chill comes down. We're telling jokes into the dark, passing around the late-night junk food, laughing till we're sore, as one after another drops exhausted into sleep. This place—the jagged cedars and firs, the sounds of animals in the hills, the smell of wet earth—this feels like home.

AUTUMN EQUINOX. THE FIRST NIGHT. A large circle of friends and strangers stand around the sacred fire that will burn for four days and four nights. The damp British Columbia night licks at our backs. Mist and woodsmoke hang over the field like ghosts. Anyone who leaves the fire is swallowed up in the mist and disappears. Above the mist, teepee poles stretch into the dark sky like old bones, glistening with dew in the moonlight. Coyotes yip from the hills. We lean in close to hear the soft voices of the elders, steady, calming, water running over stones in a stream. They tell us that the ancestors are close, and that if we listen, we can hear them speaking to us.

Abruptly, I remember: not my ancestors. My ancestors are Irish Catholic, and this tradition traces a line in my husband's family history, not mine. We are at this gathering because of David's desire to learn more about his ancestors. I don't even know where to find my ancestors, so how would they know where to find me? The cedar, the blackberries that grow like weeds, the salmon, the Fraser River—all run through the blood of the Stó:lō people around me, and through the blood of their ancestors. I don't know what runs through the blood of my ancestors—what kind of trees, what kind of food, what kind of place. I've lived in this valley for three years. Three years is not long enough to make a place your home. Is twenty? A hundred? Three hundred?

The second night. It's been an unseasonably hot day. Our crew of helpers have spent the day pouring paper cups of water for people doing ceremonies under the glare of the sun, cutting fish heads for soup, keeping children occupied, dishing out lunch. All day, David has been a blur of motion. As one of the organizers of the gathering, he has taken on the role of keeping the site running smoothly. I catch his black ponytail flying against his white T-shirt as he runs across the field, having rigged some tarps for extra shade, to dig a hole to properly bury consecrated items. By the end of the weekend, he will have earned the nickname Hole-digger. He smiles and waves, looking radiantly happy, his skin a healthy bronze.

My neck and shoulders are sunburned, and I'm relieved the sun has finally gone down. David and some of the other men are preparing for a men's sweat lodge ceremony that will probably last late into the night. I'm alone in the teepee, wondering if I should start a small fire. My sunburn is keeping me heated now, but in a couple of hours, the air temperature will take a plunge that won't stop till dawn.

Before bed, I go to the central fire to listen to the elders. Elder Mary, who most people call Grandmother, speaks about remembering our ancestors and where we came from. "Don't be ashamed of who you are," she says. I feel as if I'm trespassing, watching from a distance something private that doesn't apply to me. It applies to David, who didn't acknowledge his Native ancestry till he was twenty-five years old. But as I walk away from the fire, feeling the night chill envelop me, the phrase returns—"Don't be ashamed of who you are"—and I realize I am ashamed. I have been walking around here, trying to make myself as invisible as my red hair and freckles permit. I don't know exactly what I am ashamed of; I just know that my own history is layered into this one I so admire in a way that makes it difficult to feel proud.

Third day. All weekend I have carried around this sense that people are looking into my soul and can see the feelings of guilt I'm hiding there. David teases me about my Catholic guilt. I can't even imagine what it's like to believe that all your private thoughts are truly private. Around three o'clock in the afternoon, the splitting headache that has been slowly building all day suddenly overwhelms me, and I have to go into the teepee and lie down. The pain grows so thick and intense I can't speak. It may be sunstroke, since I'm not prone to headaches. When glasses of water and cool cloths fail to soothe it, a Stó:lō man named Joe comes in with a juniper smudge. He speaks gently. "You're all blocked up. Are you worried about something? Maybe wondering what you're doing lying in a teepee with this strange guy waving smoke over you?" He's quiet for a minute. The juniper smoke is pungent and sharp. Behind closed eyelids, I'm drifting. "You know, we're all related anyways," he says. I wonder if I'm delirious. I haven't said a word.

That night by the fire, Joe finds me and presses a bundle into my hands. "This has been in my family a long time," he says. "I want you to have it." Then he disappears into the dark. He has given me a woven turquoise cloth, trimmed around the edge with black and printed with four black West Coast eagle designs, one in each corner. I think of Joe's earlier words and see them now as more than just a pep talk for a young white woman who's having a hard time fitting in. What am I worried about? And what makes me want to belong here? This gift has made me want to know the answers.

On the last night, a few of us linger. Tomorrow we have to return to jobs, electric lights, and the strange, distant language of the everyday. David and I have even more reason to be reluctant to leave. In three days, we'll load our belongings into a 1965 Valiant and a 1981 Scirocco, and with a cat in each car for company, we'll move ourselves over the mountains and into the claustrophobic emptiness of Saskatchewan.

We're leaving so that David can get his university degree at Saskatchewan Indian Federated College, the only college of its kind in Canada. We're leaving behind our little rented house on a mountain acreage, set in among giant cedars, firs, and maples. The smell outside our kitchen window on a fall day is of baking fir cones and needles and the sweet, warm rot of fallen leaves. Up on the mountain, we watched eagles riding the thermals up from the valley floor, circling in broad, still sweeps without moving their wings. A baby bear once walked through our yard, shaking his wet fur. Deer appear in the early morning fog, nibbling at branches near the house. Our second winter, the pond froze long enough to be cleared for one night of skating in the moonlight. For David, we are leaving his home, since he has lived in British Columbia all his life and so have his ancestors, as far back as anyone can remember. For me, it is another move in a long string of moves.

WHILE WE PACK AWAY the blankets, food, wash basins, and tarps, our friends are in the woods preparing a sweat for us. The sun has dropped below the trees when we remove our rings, hair ties, and earrings and put them on a mound outside the lodge with other precious belongings. At twilight, we slip through a crack in the earth and disappear.

In the moist pitch-dark, I am laid low by heat. I push aside blankets to find a cool spot of mud to lay my cheek on. Outside noises are distant and muffled: feet pounding the dirt, coyotes yowling.

This symbolism rings in the body, does not need to be untwisted by the machinations of the mind. This is not some strange ritual where you strike your breast three times, saying, "Oh, Lord, I am not worthy. . . . In the name of the Father, the Son and the Holy Ghost," taking on your tongue a flat wafer of pasty flour that's supposed to be bread that's supposed to be the body of this Christ whose father saw fit to let him be hammered through the fragile flesh and veins of his palms and feet. I always had a hard time understanding what that had to do with love.

At intervals, we surface and douse ourselves with shocking cold water from a barrel.

Afterwards, we sit around the fire and eat: hot chili, potato salad, buns, dark oily salmon, taco chips, salty black olives, and lots of rich coffee made in shifts in a fire-blackened espresso pot, and thickened with evaporated milk. The sparks from our fire twist into the September night.

We are as fresh as babies, washed of the guilt, the embarrassment, the pain of adulthood. We linger in the woods, suspecting that this charm will dissipate as soon as we leave here. Our conversation goes like this:

"Any more of that coffee?"

"I can make more."

"Pass the olives, please."

"Chips?"

Finally, we have to go. The wet grass and cars, when we leave the woods, are shrouded in mist. It forms our cover

as we slip behind steering wheels. It is 4 a.m. when we
drive out of it, heading home.

OUR HOME ON THE MOUNTAINSIDE, which we would
leave in three days, overlooked the reservation where
David's mother grew up. David's mother's family married
into the Stó:lō nation, this sprawling territory of First
Nations reserves strung along the Fraser River valley like
floats on a fishing net. Tucked in among the prime real
estate and gated communities of the Chilliwack area,
David's reserve clusters in pockets at the foot of Mount
Cheam, in the Coast Mountains.

Mary, a Shuswap elder, had lived for more than forty
years in the Stó:lō nation. Mary and David's friendship
began a few years earlier, when another friend introduced
them; Mary chatted about David's relatives as if he'd lived
on his reserve all his life. But he had never lived there, so
she patiently taught him things about the culture she
thought he should know. He wasn't the only one. Mary
visited the prisons and taught prisoners about the sweat
lodge. She spoke at schools and held circle meetings on
reserves around Stó:lō. As you drove the winding, cedar-
lined road through her reserve, a large white teepee rose
from her property like the snow-capped mountain peaks
that surround the valley, welcoming anyone who wanted
to learn.

The first time I met Mary, David and I had gone out to
her house to help cut up a deer that someone had brought
to her. Her home was quintessential grandmother,

crowded with a lifetime of things saved because they might come in handy: collections of buttons, balls of yarn, neatly folded fabric stacked on shelves, ribbons, books, carefully straightened twist-ties in clean jars, tightly rolled plastic grocery bags, and jars of medicines like dried cedar and juniper berries. Engagements crowded the calendar on her fridge, and her answering machine picked up a steady stream of messages. About six of us worked quietly in the small kitchen, draining pot after pot of coffee as we cut the big slabs of meat into neat little packages, ready for the freezer. Though Mary was in her seventies, she sat down only for the occasional smoke. The rest of the time, she busied herself filling the sink with hot, soapy water to wash knives that needed to be sharpened, checking our work, and supervising the young man cutting the big carcass on the back porch. In that kitchen, up to my elbows with smears of blood and speckles of gristle and bone chips, I felt light. I felt free of the low-grade apprehension that dogged me like a stray cat through most of my day-to-day interactions with other people. I felt respected, without anyone expecting me to say anything to demonstrate how worthy I was. Not a power kind of respect, just a simple, ordinary respect for being human.

The work parties became my favourite times with Mary. Hot afternoons splitting wood to sputtering, chainsaw-buzz accompaniment: place the wood on the block, stand back, raise the axe, drive it in. Sweat running through a dusting of dirt and sawdust. Muscles feeling a slow burn. Stacking wood: turn, reach for the wood being passed to you, fit it into the stack, turn. Sewing cloth on the frame of the sweat lodge: needle in, pull it tight, needle out, adjust the cloth, needle in. The cadence of the work emptied my mind and loosened my body, like a dammed-up creek that finally works its way clear of the debris and runs again.

I began to notice the difference between the ease I felt swinging rhythmically through the long, hot days of our work parties and the tight knot of anxiety that normally choked me up. In my normal life, there was a loneliness so commonplace that it was invisible; I thought that almost everyone felt it, but no one acknowledged it. If someone passed me in the carpeted, air-conditioned hall at the college where I worked, asking, "How are you?" what if I said, "Last night I woke up at 2 a.m. and heard the coyotes wailing in the cedar woods across the road. I walked into the kitchen and saw moonlight washing the grass in the backyard with silver. I watched David sleeping, his eyelashes as long and black as little bird feathers. The pulse in his neck was so delicate. I cried because I missed my mother." What if I said, "I just logged off my computer and I'm going to get in my car, roll down all the windows, and drive into a different time zone." Or what if I said, "How are *you*? At work you're motivated, goal-oriented, a self-starter, think outside the box. But last night I saw you at the Safeway checkout with your TV dinners and your *TV Guide*, sadness clinging to you like thick, grey cobwebs."

Mary said, "Everything we do is a prayer," and though it wasn't a kind of prayer I was familiar with, I felt a glimmer of what she meant by that. Straddling a roof in the sunshine, passing tools back and forth, pounding out a song with our hammers, I recognized the absence of the loneliness and felt grateful.

MARY OFTEN DEBATED about whether to write down the details of things like ceremonies and traditional practices. Her passion for the power of the culture made her seriously consider it. She knew I wrote, so when we sat in her neat little living room, she explained to me why she thought writing these things down was a mistake. "People go out and buy these books," she said, fishing a copy of a thick green paperback with a New Age title from under her coffee table. "They read about the four directions. They read about how to do a sweat. Then they think they know these things. You don't learn about it just by reading a book. You don't learn about it in a weekend, where you go and pay some money to somebody who read a book. You don't even learn about it in a year. These things take time." For her, it was a lifetime of work. She'd been seriously ill as a child, and when she'd recovered, the elders took her on as an apprentice. She learned about plant medicines and how to use them. And she learned how to cross into what the Celts called the Otherworld, and what to do once she got there.

If things were written down, they could be twisted, she told me, by people who didn't understand them. Then they would really be lost, tangled in a swamp of misinterpretation.

"If it's written in a book," she told me, "people think they don't need to remember. That's what happened with your people. They can't hold anything in their memories any more."

That truth was evidenced in Ireland in 1922. During the transfer of power from the British to the Irish provisional government, the Public Record Office in Dublin became a battleground. The PRO contained a huge treasury of government records from all over Ireland, records that would help someone like me in the painstaking process of reconstructing a family history. Two weeks after the PRO was handed over to the provisional government, renegades occupied the building and set up a bomb factory in the records treasury. In the ensuing attempt to recapture it, a violent explosion scattered charred bits of records for miles around. In his book *The Irish Roots Guide*, Tony McCarthy writes, "In a matter of seconds, two heavy mines, which had exploded in the records treasury, destroyed seven centuries of work."

Of course, the oral tradition of remembering is subject to perils too. In Canada, the government devised methods only slightly more subtle than bombs to destroy oral records and stories. David's paternal grandmother was Kwakwaka'wakw, from Alert Bay on the coast of British Columbia. She was born in 1913 and named Kesaguila, after her grandmother. But in 1918, nuns at an Anglican residential school renamed her Alice. In a CBC interview conducted in 1965, she wondered why the Scottish and Japanese and Chinese were still allowed to do their dances while the Indians were prevented from doing "their own celebrating."

"We were told not to have anything to do with it," she says. "In this school, we were told it was wicked. We weren't supposed to; we were supposed to forget all that. That's what we were in school for, to try and forget it, not to remember it any more, because it was wicked."

"What was wicked?" the interviewer asks her.

"I don't know what was wicked, but it was supposed to be wicked [laughs], whatever it was."

WE WERE ON THE TRANS-CANADA, headed east to Saskatchewan. The mountains were covered in long shadows now. It was spitting rain. The light was that worse-than-dark, washed-out murk, the time when elk and deer out for a suppertime stroll get creamed by drivers taken totally by surprise when their bulk suddenly materializes in the middle of the road. I hadn't wanted to go through Roger's Pass in the dark, but our plan was to stop in Golden for supper, then decide if we wanted to drive on or not. So I kept driving. I led the way in the Valiant, only because David's Scirocco had an undiagnosed electrical problem that made his headlights cast only a dim glow. He stayed close behind me, watching my tail lights.

Just about at Roger's Pass, the few drops of rain turned into a deluge. My windshield wipers, with only one speed, could barely keep up. At the speed limit, eighty kilometres an hour (or fifty miles an hour on my old speedometer), on single-lane, unfamiliar, serpentine highway, I felt I was going too fast for comfort. But a long string of impatient traffic was piling up behind us. My cat, who had been calmly purring under the driver's seat so far, seemed to sense my tension. She climbed out and started pacing on the back of my seat, watching over my shoulder. Then she climbed into the back window and huddled there, perfectly blocking my vision of the traffic behind me.

I took my eyes off the road for a second to reach for a thin, curved piece of wild rosewood that was on my dashboard. Mary had given both David and me pieces of the wood and told us to put them on the front and rear dash of our cars. Rosewood seemed to be the Shuswap St. Christopher's medal, protecting travellers from harm. A small eagle feather I'd been given at the gathering was tied to my rear-view mirror, along with a few unidentified feathers that the previous owner of the Valiant had collected. Also on the rear-view mirror hung a favourite, very old turquoise-coated crucifix medal with Jesus, the Virgin Mary, St. Christopher, and the baby Jesus on the four arms. I travelled alone in Mexico and Guatemala with that medal pinned to the pocket of my jean jacket. It had been given to my mother when she was a child.

Lodged on one end of the dash was a round, pink-veined white stone like some tiny human organ, and beside it, a shiny hunk of quartz and a grey rock wrinkled like a petrified animal dropping. On the other end of the dash was a smooth green river rock from the Chilliwack River, a couple of perfectly smooth twists of driftwood, and a luminous purple seashell. If I made a sudden sharp turn, all my objects would go sliding to one end of the dash. I prided myself on being able to drive the Valiant down the seven-mile mountain road where we had lived near Chilliwack without spilling a single rock. But I always knew when David had been driving the car, because the dashboard would be completely bare and I'd have to go hunting under the seat for my rocks.

These objects were amulets to me; I'd often pick one up and rub it in my sweaty hand when I was under stress. I had collected stones since I was a kid and from time to time carried one around with me as a good-luck charm. When I was working on my master's degree, a friend who rode in my car for the first time saw my rocks and dug in his pocket for his own sweat-smooth black stone he carried everywhere. When I met Mary, she explained that stones, like eagle feathers, can be sacred. The objects themselves are not worshipped, but they are acknowledged for the power they hold. They can be called upon for strength or comfort or protection during a crisis.

Learning that about rocks seemed to be a confirmation of something I already sensed. It might have been a habit I picked up in the Catholic Church, where the "contemplation of sacred icons" is distinguished from the "worshipping of false idols." When we were kids, my sisters and I collected holy cards and medals like some kids collect hockey cards. For a special occasion, like Christmas or First Communion or a birthday, my mother or grandmother or aunt, or maybe one of the many nuns who were friends of my mother's, would give us small 2-by-4-inch cards that pictured the Virgin Mary, the Nativity scene, or a popular saint carrying out the activity he or she was famous for. Sometimes we were given a medal, usually of the Virgin Mary or Jesus, or a rosary. I liked the rosaries purely for decorative reasons; they came in plastic cut into diamond-edged sparkles and colours like pearly pink, ruby red, clear.

A 1940s Catholic catechism of my mother's tries to put the honouring of saints' images and holy objects in proper perspective: "We do not pray to the images or relics of the saints, but to the persons they represent." A 1995 catechism shows the Church still trying to get a grip on the common Catholic practice of collecting holy objects. The "beauty of the images" is meant to "move [us] to contemplation, as a meadow delights the eyes and subtly infuses the soul with the Glory of God." But as millions of Catholics from Mexico to Portugal know, a holy medal or a plastic Jesus on the dash is a good-luck charm.

With my rosewood in my lap, my mind was briefly taken off the string of headlights I saw curving behind me in my side mirror as I rounded bends. We reached a passing lane, and suddenly the black bulk of a 4-by-4 truck was beside me streaming rain. The driver kept pace with the Valiant long enough to blast his horn at me for holding him back in traffic. I held steady at the speed limit as the traffic poured past me. I had to keep wiping my sweaty palms on my pant legs. Where was Golden? The cat moved enough so that I could see David in the rear-view mirror again. Then I saw a sign: Golden 12 km. As I tried to convert miles to kilometres to calculate how long it would take me to get there when I was going fifty miles an hour, I picked up a song being tapped out by the noisy rhythms inside my car. I don't have a radio. But once, I had heard the whole chorus of "Heart of Gold" in the hum, slap, knock, knock, knock of engine and body noises of the Valiant. Now it was the eagle song we'd sung again and again around a drum at the gathering. I listened, shook my head to clear it, then heard the song more clearly than ever: a steady drum beat, a rising and falling of melody. I drove into the Husky station in Golden a little calmer.

LATER THAT NIGHT in a Golden motel, still feeling shaky from the road, I thought about the phenomenon of the "wannabe." Like Margo Kane writes, "Cherokee, Pawnee, Comanche, Wannabe." I think what I am is a "wanna-have." I have culture envy. I envy people who have a place, and stories and a culture that grew out of that place. I'm native Canadian, but not indigenous; of Irish origin, but not Irish. Catholicism is as close as I come to a tradition, but it's not connected to a place. It's funny in a perverse kind of way that European colonizers worked so diligently to destroy aboriginal traditions, but a couple hundred years later, the colonizers' great-grandchildren, overwhelmingly, know next to nothing about their own traditions.

Saskatchewan will be the fourth province I've lived in. When people ask me where I'm from, I sort through possible answers: childhood in Ontario, teenage and university years in Winnipeg, a chunk of my adult life in B.C. There is no family farm I return to every holiday. I'm like the immigrant with the hard-to-pronounce name who would rather be called Jane. Sure it's my history, but I don't feel like trying to make sense of it every time a stranger wants to engage me in small talk. I'm a migrant Canadian. Home is the place I've left behind.

2.
BEGINNING

. . . The moon carved unknown totems
out of the lakeshore
owls in the beardusky woods derided him
moosehorned cedars circled his swamps and tossed
their antlers up to the stars.

—EARLE BIRNEY, "BUSHED"

MY SISTER PAT HANDED ME a manila envelope so fat it wouldn't close. On the front she had written "Mother's stuff."

"This was in her desk," Pat said. "I've been meaning to do something with it. Some of her notes go back to the sixties."

"I didn't even know she was collecting that stuff," I said.

"Neither did I," said Pat.

It was April, the spring after our move, and I was in

North Vancouver picking up some of the books and records we'd stored at Pat's house. April, and it was pouring rain, had rained steadily all day. With the towering cedar trees up on the mountain, the sky never really lightened into day. I spent the morning and afternoon drinking tea at the dining-room table with the lights on, waiting for my day to begin, then easing into the close of it with Pat and her husband, John, still thinking I should do something like brush my hair.

The rain I didn't miss. The only thing familiar about it was the low-grade depression I used to feel almost daily, as I walked a mile with my gumboots and umbrella through the steady downpour from the cheap parking to my classes at UBC. With other Prairie students, I reminisced about Winnipeg nights so hot you couldn't sleep, and about summer storms building slowly all afternoon, then hitting with a vengeance, ripping limbs off trees, flooding streets in minutes. Prairie rain had some passion to it. At least that's how I remembered it when I lived in B.C.

David and my first two months in Regina—September and October—cast both of us into a funk. The sky stayed relentlessly grey. A cold wind blew the trees bare in a day. The grass had already turned a pale, non-descript brown. Everything had a monochromatic greyness to it. We slept and worried about our rented house having sick-building syndrome. I longed for September in the Fraser Valley, the best month of the whole year—sunshine every day, leaves turning, crisp nights, fires in the woodstove.

In North Vancouver that night, we had a family dinner with my sister Barbie and her family, and my dad. The other half of the family—two sisters and a brother—now lived in Winnipeg, where we'd moved from Southern Ontario when I was ten. Around the table, I went over the details of the trip I was planning for next month.

"I'm going to research our family a bit, find out where they came from, stuff like that. I'll go to Ontario first, then to Ireland."

I didn't say, "I'm looking for a culture for myself." I had tried that out on some friends, and they said, "What is that supposed to mean? This is your culture. All around you."

"You mean like Slurpees and Rambo?"

"Sure. You may not like it, but it's yours."

But it didn't feel like mine at all, and neither did the kitschy Canadiana they collected half ironically—maple leaf salt and pepper shakers, royal family tea towels, RCMP plates, Group of Seven art books—revelling in the shallowness of it. Why wasn't that good enough for me? Only because it didn't ring one clink of recognition.

So to avoid being plied with questions I couldn't answer yet, I took refuge in the genealogy explanation, knowing I had almost no interest in pursuing dates and birth certificates. But I felt a sense of obligation, since I would be the first family member to go to Ireland, to produce something concrete, some ancient family signature on some ancient family document—something.

My mother's notes, though, contained far more information than I had imagined. After dessert, I pulled out the

papers and spread them on the table. There was the
turquoise ink of Mother's favourite fountain pen and her
cramped, slanted handwriting.

"Her writing looks just like yours," Barbie said to me.

"It looks like yours, Barbie," said Pat.

"Let's see that," said my dad. I handed it over. He
looked at it and was quiet.

There was a thick family genealogy a distant relative
had started. There were some yellow, crumbling newspaper clippings and letters to my mother from relatives
that began: "Since you asked me to write down what I
could remember about the family . . ." The letters were
dated from the sixties and seventies. A few pages of grid
paper mapped out direct descendants on both her side and
my father's. There were typed pages too, the black letters
fuzzy from carbon copying, listing ancestors' names,
birthdates and death dates, places of birth, and a few
details in parentheses, such as (cooper by trade) (worked
Alaska Highway). A list of the Smiths documented the
various ways people had died: killed when horse and
buggy overturned; drowned age two; killed overseas; died
at three or four, fever; killed by streetcar. We used to tease
my mother about her fascination with the way people had
died.

"She always dropped her pronouns and prepositions,"
Barbie said. "That came from making all those lists."

My mother left a trail of lists through the house and
through the day, mostly task lists of various categories:
farm chores, garden priorities, social occasions. There

were shopping lists with cryptic shorthand words like
"mush.", "pot.", "T.S." When my sisters and I did the
shopping, we'd end up buying three items to cover the T.P.
code on her list—toilet paper, toothpaste, and tomato
paste.

"Remember the list of neighbours at the farm?" Barbie
said. When we first moved out to the farm east of
Winnipeg, my mother made a list of important neighbours:

   Ruchkalls (flowers)
   Reimers (eggs)
   Christies (cows)
   McDermotts (pigs)

My brother-in-law Mike saw that list one Sunday while
he and my sister Mary were out at the farm, drinking tea
at the dining-room table. "I see you've written down your
impressions of your new neighbours," he had said.

"That wasn't Mike," said Pat now, as she collected
dirty plates.

"Mike wouldn't have said that to your mother," my
dad said.

"Sure he would have," said Barbie's husband, Steve,
laughing and setting my dad just slightly on edge. Steve
had been a part of the family a long time, and he used to
trade irreverent jabs with my mom at family gatherings.
But my mother's low-key sense of humour wasn't part of
my dad's memory of her. He had formed his own reverent
history of my mother, and images I had, like her on the

phone to friends, laughing so hard she had to take off her glasses and wipe her eyes, didn't fit.

"I'm sure it was Mike," I said. "Unless it was Mary. I was there."

"Photographic memory, eh?" said Steve. And when I laughed, he said, "Ah, you have your mother's laugh."

The Smith sickly laugh, as Steve calls it, a half-hearted laugh that means I know you think you're funny, so I'll humour you.

Other things I inherited from my mother:

- A handiness with tools. She could rewire a lamp or hammer together a cold frame for early tomatoes. The images in TV shows like "I Love Lucy" and "The Flintstones," where the women nagged their husbands to do repairs, didn't apply in our house. I have a memory of my mother about thirty feet up an extension ladder, painting the eavestroughs, perfectly at ease. In fact, she's holding the paintbrush at a jaunty angle and casually leaning out from the ladder, looking down at our new Falcon station wagon and continuing the argument we were having about the colour. "From up here it looks white." (It was supposed to be powder blue.)
- No fear of heights. I climbed the same beams she did in my grandparents' barn, taunting my little brother, Neil, to try it, pointing out the upturned prongs of the hay rake waiting underneath.
- Her hands. Freckled, knobby knuckles, three promi-

nent bones branching out like crow's feet, blue veins close to the surface. I wear the eternity ring my father gave her on their twenty-fifth anniversary. One morning not long after I put it on, I woke up and was startled by the familiar, comforting hand on my pillow, which turned out to be my own.

- An ability to sew. And enjoy it. She spent stray hours bent over the 1960 Singer, sewing curtains, quilts, clothes for herself and for us. I still think about the creamy yellow high-school graduation gown with spaghetti straps she made me, and wonder how she was able to find a pattern and fabric that an eighteen-year-old would approve of. I don't remember helping with it, but I remember learning to sew when I was about seven and mowing a clean line right across my best friend's index finger. Like my mother, I can get lost in sewing now, a meditation in fitting together pieces, tucking away ragged edges on her old Singer.
- A need for lists.

Mother left a kind of diary of her last year, actually a collection of lists. When she found out she had cancer, she kept notes in a pocket calendar, lists of symptoms, medications taken, foods tolerated. And lists for a picnic she was planning just two months before she died. Her two brothers, Jack and Neil, and their wives, Joan and Sylvia, came out from Ontario. The picnic lists covered groceries to buy, foods to prepare ahead of time, things to bring to the park. I flipped through the pages of the calendar again and again, looking for some clue, some way in beyond the "apple sauce, tom. soup, milk—O.K.; picnic ham, pot. salad, juice—cranberry?" The calendar is frustrating for everything it leaves out. Like the family genealogy, it is just a skeleton with ghostly gaps whistling between the bones.

In a genealogical centre, I was given this advice: to place myself at the beginning of things. Write my name on the bottom centre of the chart. The family tree grows out from there, like a funnel, the generations pouring into me. I struggle to fit all the branches onto one page. By generation three, I'm already running off the edges, scrunch up the paper, start again with a bigger piece. I want something compact and orderly, one page I can pack neatly into the side pocket of my backpack.

Back in Regina, I cashed in my RRSP and started packing. I had an 18-by-13-inch backpack. I wanted to be unencumbered. Once, catching a ferry to Morocco, I tripped over a curb; the sudden jar of my overloaded pack dislocated my back, so I left the pack in the ferry station lockers and went to Morocco for a month with only a daypack that held a toothbrush, a journal, and a not-quite-complete change of clothes. Since then, I've tried to come close to that feeling of freedom I had on the bus switchbacking through the Atlas Mountains, as I realized I didn't need any of it. For this trip, I started with one pair of chinos, one pair of shorts, one sleeveless summer dress, a light wool sweater, a T-shirt, a long-sleeved shirt, my

Swiss Army knife, and underwear. I searched the city's sporting goods stores for tubes of Coghlan soap, a biodegradable soap that can be used for dishes, hair, face, and clothes. Then I thought maybe I was going too far. By the time six weeks was up, my hair would be like straw. I put in a travel-size bottle of shampoo. The things that started to weigh me down were the paper goods: maps, notebooks, guidebook, pleasure reading.

David was taking summer classes, so he wasn't coming with me. But even if he hadn't had commitments, even if we could have found the extra money for his plane ticket, we both thought this was a trip I should make alone. I was on a quest, and a quest is meant to be a difficult journey through an unfamiliar landscape. With David along, I knew it would not be difficult or unfamiliar enough. I would take refuge in his company, sleep late, have drawn-out brunches, probably splurge on hotels we couldn't afford, and end up having to cut the trip short. This was another fact that I didn't bother trying to explain to anyone else. I was travelling with a sense of purpose so serious it embarrassed me a little. If I failed to fulfil my purpose, to find the object of my quest, only I had to know about it. To everyone else, I would have had a holiday in the homeland of my ancestors, with lots of green landscape photos to back me up.

HAVING LIVED IN THE WESTERN PROVINCES for twenty-odd years, I'd forgotten how beautiful Southern Ontario was—big maples shading the streets, lilacs and elegant old

buildings, homes with front porches and intricate wood-
work around the red brick, softly rolling hills and
graperies. It was the kind of beauty that made me imagine
a life of sitting on a front porch, taking afternoon tea and
reading novels while the children play croquet on the lawn.
It had an irrevocably tamed feeling, unlike the Prairies,
with their cheap strip malls and boxy wooden houses that
seem like they could be swept away by a few hard winds.
Or British Columbia, where it feels like the place is going
to be eaten up every spring by encroaching vines, blackberries, and alders that spring up like dandelions.

This part of Ontario won't be reclaimed by nature.
Catharine Parr Traill, when she saw this part of the world
in 1832, reflected that "still there is a great portion of
forest standing which it will take years of labour to
remove." But the European settlers set to the place with a
passion to subdue it, to clip it and plough it and hew it
into a less threatening shape, a shape that looked more
like home. Every account I read of early settlers in
Ontario laments the trees, in one way or another. The
trees were a beautiful menace, lush, wild, out of control.
Set down in the thick of "the bush," the settlers had to
hack out a home, tree by tree. I imagined the eagerness to
"civilize the wilderness" that so many settler diaries
mention. Surrounded by trees—pine, maple, beech, white
ash, cherry, basswood—behind you a tent, ahead of you a
long, fierce winter, you wet your hands for a good grip on
the axe and take a swing. The blade pings off the hard-
wood and leaves a tiny nick in the trunk. You look around

at the trees crowded in upon you; you hear your baby crying from the tent, and you have to lean against the tree to stop yourself from crumpling to your knees and sobbing. Thank God your wife can't see your face. You take a deep breath and swing again.

A wealthy man could hire people to do the work. Thomas Magrath, writing to his father-in-law in Ireland, the Reverend Thomas Radcliff, describes the clearing of the unsightly growth from his land in the bush. Ironically, while most settlers battle the trees to clear enough land to make room for their farms, Magrath dismisses the native trees as offending his good taste: "I have planted three thousand trees, and a great variety of evergreens to conceal our offices, and for ornament: for in truth the trees about us of natural growth are far from pleasing in their appearance, their closeness preventing the lateral furnishing of the branches, so essential to beauty."

My perspective is skewed as I drive through here as an adult, with four rubber tires between me and the earth, passing neatly painted craft shops, tea rooms, and markets. For the first ten years of my life, I lived here in a smaller, wilder world. Under the wooden ramp leading into the second storey of my grandparents' barn, my brother and I played, hidden by elderberry bushes and sumach trees. The cool mud wafted a pungent skunk smell, rotting rags, and mildew. Our parents' warnings of tramps who slept in the hayloft and tossed their empty whisky bottles under the ramp whispered through the hairs on our arms. The chaotic world under there drew us, as to something thrilling and opposite to the comforting sound of the lawn mower humming through our screened bedroom window on summer evenings and the delicious scent of barbecue starter fuel.

At a big vegetable garden down beside the Twelve Mile Creek, at a place we called Jackson Flats, my mother grew tomatoes, potatoes, corn, and beans. We already had a garden, a field of corn, and fruit trees at our home on Pelham Road, so the produce grown at the Flats was to sell at our fruit-and-vegetable stand. The stand brought in a bit of extra money, but mostly my mother did it because she liked the work, the methodical patience it required, the dash of experimentation. Potatoes liked to grow between the beans and the corn. Tomatoes were said to grow best in the same spot year after year. We surrounded them with a line of marigolds to keep bugs away. Potato bugs could be knocked off the leaves with a stick, into a can of soapy water. Wood ashes would keep slugs away from the beans.

She also liked the garden because she liked to be outside. In a letter to a friend in 1976, about five years after we'd moved away from the Niagara Peninsula farm, she wrote, half-joking, "I got to get back to the land." Working in the rich creekside dirt, she sometimes stopped and told us, "Look at the colour of that." Six kids between the ages of five and thirteen dotted the freshly dug garden, each with a task, making rows or running the seeder along the furrows. My oldest sister, Anne, had the plum job of driving the tractor and bringing the lunch. She found excuses to make trips back up to the house for more Freshie, a stack of bushel baskets, Band-Aids for bloodsucker wounds. I don't know that any of us shared my mother's enthusiasm for the colour of the soil, but we loved going to the Flats. The gravel road to get there dropped steeply from the sunny paved highway. The tidy farms disappeared suddenly from the rear-view mirror, and the car slipped through a tunnel of trees, down to the cool earth spread out beside the creek. When we weren't planting or pulling weeds, we swam in the slow, muddy creek shaded by trees. There were no lists of rules posted here about spitting or running, no other kids to splash you, no fences marking a boundary. A big rock protruded from the middle of the creek, and you could stretch out on it like a lizard and watch the sunlight coming through the canopy of leaves, making unreal little white sparkles on the water, turning it into something alive. Under the water lurked tadpoles, frogs, bloodsuckers, maybe snakes, some painted turtles. You tried not to think about them when you swam.

As an adult, I have recurring dreams about the Flats. I travel deep into the shade of the trees that close over me like a cave, and along the water to warm pools, comforting as a womb.

Now when I look for the familiar chaotic places of my childhood, I can't find them. The road to the Flats is a dead end with a No Trespassing sign, a barbed-wire fence, and nothing familiar beyond it. I drive down winding Pelham Road, past our old house, remembering my

mother's outrage when she found out that the people who
bought the place tore out her rose gardens and replaced
them with chunks of driftwood. Or maybe the roses had
just died from neglect, which probably wouldn't have
occurred to her, since she deadheaded and watched for
bugs as a matter of habit on her way into the house with
groceries. She had planted a rose bush for each of us kids
when we were born. Mine was a soft mauve, the most
fragrant of the bunch. Her own favourite was the sunset-
coloured Peace. The rose bushes are still gone, but so is
the driftwood. Just past our old house, separated by rows
of grapes, my grandparents' farm, a "century farm," sits
solid and orderly, occupied by strangers now.

By the time I was born, my grandfather had stopped
serious farming. He still kept a few cows and sold grapes.
My uncle Neil worked around the farm when he had
time to come home, but my grandfather wasn't up to the
physical work any more. Since my grandmother taught
elementary school in Niagara Falls, the farm was probably suffering a little from neglect, although I didn't see it
that way at the time. It was the neglect we kids loved.
Stairs led up to the attic in the farmhouse, where sun
streamed through the dust. We dug through the boxes of
magazines and tins of spices my grandmother had saved.
In the barn, under seasons of compacted hay dust and
binder twine, we discovered the ring to a trap door we
thought we were the first to find. The trap door led to the
dank ground floor, where cows used to live. By then,
cobwebs had grown thick over the stall doors and the

rusty farm tools hanging on nails. After my grandparents died, my uncle took on the task of putting the farm back to work.

Beyond the farm is a place I'd been looking forward to going to: the old family cemetery where we used to play. It hid in untended little woods on the original land that my ancestors first cleared. Someone, maybe my grandfather, had told us not to go in there, that it was a fairy ring. And if a horse or cow ever wandered in, they wouldn't follow it; they'd just wait for it to come out. Tantalized by that inexplicable story, we used to leave our bikes in the ditch and walk across the field to the clump of woods. In the shadows of the trees, under layers of moss and fallen leaves, we uncovered broken bits of moss-blackened family tombstones, with weeds pushing up through the cracks. We could sit there on the damp earth and imagine a time when the world was so contained in one place that you buried your dead relatives in the backyard, like we did with our cats that got run over by cars on Pelham Road. An old smell hung in there, musty and neglected like the old pieces of bottles we sometimes dug up. Ghosts rustled their long black dresses in the trees and snagged dusty cloth on branches. Sometimes we ran shrieking from them. We plunged from the dankness of the woods into the yellow summer light and the clover field, alive with bees and insects, like we were waking up disoriented from an afternoon nap we didn't mean to have.

I expect the place to be changed, and it is. The cleaned and repaired tombstones are laid in a neat row, surrounded by trimmed lawn and bordered by only a few of the old trees. The cemetery is a quaint little piece of Ontario settler heritage now, lending ambience to my relatives' prosperous new estate vineyard. I fleetingly begrudge my relatives their progress. I can't imagine any ghosts of mine living here.

My uncles still live in the area. Uncle Neil had moved recently from the century farm that was granted to my great-great-great-great-grandfather Smith for being loyal to Britain. From my mother's records, I know that most of my ancestors emigrated from Ireland around the time of the potato famine. They came from County Clare and County Armagh, County Cork and County Antrim. The exception is this Smith line on my mother's father's side. They are my earliest ancestors here, United Empire Loyalists who fled the United States around 1784, leaving behind most of their possessions. This Smith I know little about, only a first name and an approximate birthdate; no place of birth or family origins. Even the name Smith could be an anglicization from the Irish. I am hoping my uncles can tell me something.

My uncle Neil used to be a priest. My mother sometimes told us how all her girlfriends lamented that her good-looking younger brother had joined the priesthood. Sometimes in the summer, at hay-cutting time, Father Neil said Mass at my grandparents' house. My grandma bustled around the house, getting things ready. I think there were few things more exciting to my grandma than having her own son say Mass in her own house. She set glasses of orange juice and plates of cookies on the dining-

room table. In the living room, she set up a card table
draped with a white tablecloth and placed a Bible in the
centre. Father Neil was a handsome man, with curly dark
hair and a square jaw. He radiated an unhurried calm as
he took his religious paraphernalia from a black doctor's
bag and placed it on the table. There was something
strange about seeing that golden chalice in my grandma
and grandpa's ordinary living room, alongside the television set and the old tufted maroon couch. And as Uncle
Neil's soft drawl singsonged through the Mass, I noticed
a startling thing: beneath the hem of his black cassock, he
wore running shoes, green with grass stains.

Maybe the running shoes were a sign of a renegade spirit,
because in the 1960s, Uncle Neil fell in love and left the
priesthood to be married to Sylvia. Together they raised
sheep on the century farm, and kept horses and a dog. Like
my mother, he seemed to find something satisfying in the
regular, physical tasks of the farm. He continued his
involvement in the Church and wrote an occasional article
for the religion section of the weekend newspaper, quietly
raising questions about Catholicism, like the wisdom of
preventing priests from marrying. From my perspective,
his faith seemed intelligent, courageous, even a bit daring.
I told him about my plan to go to Ireland to try to find out
something about our family and our spiritual roots. He
warned me that he disliked the fervent Irish approach to
Catholicism—the self-denial and exultation of punishment. At the time, I didn't know quite what he meant, but
his words would come back to haunt me.

When I heard he went to a regular evening Mass, I
asked to go with him. I hadn't been in about ten years,
since Mother died. For several years before that, I'd gone
only on special occasions, because I knew it was important to Mother. Even now, I was driven not by a rekindled
spirituality like I'd had as a kid, but more by curiosity.
I wanted to see what, if anything, it still meant to me. I
thought that if I was going to be moved by some kind
of new awareness about the legacy I had in Catholicism,
I would feel it at St. Mary's Church, the place where
Mother had been baptized, had her First Communion,
her confirmation, and been married, then buried. But at
the last minute, I made an excuse to get out of it.
Somehow, I couldn't see myself going to Mass out of
curiosity, especially with my uncle Neil. I decided to go
to St. Mary's alone, during the day, when the church
would be empty.

I had been baptized and had my First Communion at
St. Mary's too, like most of my sisters and my brother. In
our family photo albums were several nearly indistin-
guishable group shots of rows of boys and girls on the
same church steps, the girls' gloved hands clutched in
photo-op prayer. Those steps were the first thing I noticed
when I arrived at St. Mary's. They seemed so much
smaller that I was sure they must have been replaced over
the years, because I couldn't imagine fitting all those kids
up there now.

Outside it was an unseasonably hot early June day,
thick with humidity. The grounds of the church, other

than the steps, looked exactly the same, but they were deadly quiet, just a few insects flying up from the sunny grass. I went to the grotto in the backyard, where the St. Mary's shrine was shaded by lilac bushes. A few birds chirped and poked around the stonework. I remembered I went to Brownies in the church basement and came out here to say my prayers. Maybe I prayed for help to pass my crafts test and to make it through the two painful hours before my mom would come and pick me up again. I wasn't an eager Brownie; I did it because my sisters had, and my mom let me give it up after a couple of months.

I tried the church doors, and they opened. A wave of cool, stale air enveloped me as the door clicked shut behind me. The church was empty and dim, but it smelled the same as I remembered: the pleasant scent of burnt candle wax and the slightly sour smell of old wood from the pews, an odour that became more pungent when a whole congregation sat in there in clothes damp with rain. I sat in a pew and looked up. The vaulted ceiling was painted sky blue, trimmed cleanly in white. The statue of Mary, with downcast eyes and the faintest of smiles, was the same one I had studied Sunday after Sunday, expecting to see some twitch of life, a look of approval or disapproval. She remained still, inscrutable. I glanced over at the thick red velvet curtains of the confessional. The same ones? How long would velvet last? I had a green velvet dress once. My mind wandered. It was odd to be in an empty church in the middle of a weekday. Maybe, I reasoned, that was why I felt nothing at all.

"YOU LOOK LIKE you're a long way from home," my uncle Jack said. "What's wrong?"

Actually, nothing was wrong, but it would be Uncle Jack who would notice my slightly bewildered expression, a slow-dawning "Who, me?" look that appears in so many of the old photos of me with my cousin Jody on camping trips with her dad, Uncle Jack. We were gathered at the home of my cousin Maureen, another of Uncle Jack's daughters, for a family dinner. He was my mother's older brother and about as different from Uncle Neil as two brothers could be. Uncle Jack runs closer to the Irish stereotype: fond of a pint now and then, with an easy laugh, a scorn for convention, and a supply of stories that get better with each telling.

The ones he told about my mother always seemed to involve somebody getting hurt. Like the one about their friend, also named Jack, who my mother had a "hate on" for, for some unknown reason. She was tending goal in a hockey game on the pond and made the rule that there was no high-sticking. When the puck accidentally ricocheted off Jack's skate and hit my mom in the chest, she stalked out of her net and decked Jack "clean out of his skates."

Once, at a wedding, my grandpa was out in the milk house, having a few drinks with the men, and my grandmother asked my mother to tell him they were ready to go. According to Uncle Jack, a very large woman outside the milk house scolded her to "let him have his fun."

"It's none of your business," said my mother. "I'm just telling him we're ready."

"I'd give you a slap for a nickel," she retorted.

"Well, you can take one for free," my mother snapped back.

The woman wound up and slapped her, and Mother came back with an uppercut to the chin that sent all three hundred pounds of her crashing to the ground.

Uncle Jack particularly relished these stories of his sister's temper. I'm not sure why. Maybe he wanted to make sure we didn't settle into a sanitized memory of her as some churchy lady who bore things without complaint.

At Maureen's, Uncle Jack sat in his lawn chair, looking like a more sociable version of my grandfather. He was now about the age Grandpa had been when I was growing up. Grandpa to me was a smell—pipe tobacco and headcheese—and a silent presence on babysitting duty, glued to the kitchen stool as he watched out the window and reused the same two tea bags for the whole afternoon. He wore the same faded suede windbreaker, winter or summer, often in the house. Even when he was eighty, his broad shoulders and six-foot-plus height were undiminished. My father said he had wrists like two-by-fours. We ran to him to politely ask his permission to climb on the shed roof, bathe the cats in the ditch. He nodded, rarely taking his pipe from between his teeth. Around five o'clock, he peeled potatoes and let us kids drink cold coffee. If he had ever raised his voice with any of us, we would have cowered. It was not in his nature to get excited about things.

Uncle Jack tossed out names that echoed repeatedly through the generations: Annes, Hughs, Margarets, Johns, Georges, and Catherines. To add to the confusion, both of my grandfather's parents had been Smiths. He tried to explain to me the convoluted relationships of second cousins, once or twice removed. When I tried surreptitiously to pop an antibiotic in my mouth for a sinus infection, he said, "You know sinus problems run in the Smith family." I laughed about having my head cold attributed to genes, but even this little scrap of medical history resonates with significance when you have so little to go on. Later, by accident, I happened across a notation in a book in a health-food store in downtown St. Catharines that told me that sinus problems signal blocked emotions. I believe this. Passed down through the generations and right into me, a reticence like Grandpa's that sometimes borders on the sullen. Maybe this accounts for the dearth of stories in our family.

My cousin, and childhood friend, Jody came over and sat beside her dad. She had grown into a delightful version of her mother, with lively light blue eyes and an infectious giggle.

Uncle Jack had taken Jody and me on camping trips to a lake north of Peterborough. He slept in a little trailer. Jody and I slept in the tent, and in the morning, he got up first, started the Coleman stove, and fried potatoes and the sunfish we'd caught out on the lake in a rowboat the night before. Jody and I stayed in our sleeping bags, listening to the butter crackling in the frying pan while the sun heated the thick canvas and gave off a comforting scent of oil.

"We've got some Iroquois in the family somewhere," Uncle Jack said.

"Really?" Jody and I said at the same time. This was one of those unsubstantiated family legends about the Smith origins that I'd heard bits of before. Usually it was said that you could see the heritage in Grandpa Smith's features.

"I don't know exactly where that line comes in," said Uncle Jack. "But Nicholas Smith, as you know, was a fifer in Butler's Rangers, a United Empire Loyalist. After the war, when he was settled here, he used to say, 'I'm going to see my boys.'" Those were his buddies in the Rangers, the Mohawks of Brantford. So he'd set out to walk to the Grand River area, probably forty miles of walking. The story goes that he was fluent in Iroquoian languages.

"I don't know if there's any truth to that," Uncle Neil said about the Mohawk bloodline.

"That family history Mother had says there might be a German connection," I said.

"Oh no," Uncle Neil said. "No, I don't know where that comes from. They were Irish."

He remembered his own uncle carrying around a slip of paper in his wallet to remind him of where he came from: County Donovan in Ireland, a place he'd never been. The image struck me as not only odd, but sad. What kind of homesickness is so strong it's passed on to the next generation? How lonely are you for a place to belong when you carry a name printed carefully on a scrap of paper as a reminder of a home where you've never lived?

Later, I scanned my map of Ireland. But there was no County Donovan. So, I was looking for the ancestors of a Smith, whose name might have been changed from the Irish, who probably had sinus problems and came from a non-existent county in Ireland. So much for relying on written records for our history.

AT FIRST I THOUGHT that my uncle Neil must be mistaken about this Smith being Irish. If they were Irish, I thought, would they want to be loyal to the British? But I discovered I was wrong about that. As diverse as the population in the New World, the Loyalists became Loyalists for reasons that ranged from true patriotic loyalty to simple self-interest. As the Reverend Mather Byles reflected: "Which is better—to be ruled by one tyrant three thousand miles away or by three thousand one mile away?"

The Loyalists were the first English-speaking settlers in Upper Canada. Each head of the household received a location ticket and made his way with his family past the French settlements, up the rapids of the St. Lawrence and into a wilderness "so big his mind slowed when he looked at it." Some of them had left behind well-developed farms in the States. Others had recently emigrated from Europe and missed their meadows, hedges, ivy-covered stone walls, and peaceful lanes where linnets chirped. Left on the shore with a ship-axe, a tool barely better than a hatchet, and few other tools, the families, or the men alone, had to hack their way through the thick under-brush and fallen trees, across swamps and streams, to try to locate their lots.

Capt. James Dittrick, son of a United Empire Loyalist in Butler's Rangers, the same regiment as my great-great-great-great-grandfather's, writes in his diary, "No one can tell the privations we all underwent on our first moving into the Bush. The whole country was a forrest [sic], a wilderness which had to be subdued by axe and toil. For a time we led a regular Robinson Crusoe life and with a few poles and brushwood, formed our tents on the Indian plan. As the clearances enlarged, we were supplied with some agricultural implements, for we brought nothing with us but a few seeds prepared by the careful fore-thought of the women."

The "subduing" or "civilizing" of the wilderness rings through settler narratives like a church bell. I know that this forms a big part of the heritage I carry, hauled across continents and oceans like a highly impractical and fragile set of fine china. The nineteenth-century Irish exile Thomas D'Arcy McGee wrote, "The history of our race is a history of emigration. In Asia Eden was; but beyond Eden the world lay. . . . Upon what consolation did our first parents rest? Upon labor and upon hope, 'Go forth and fill the earth and subdue it.'" In the lush Canadian wilderness, during the long, dark night of wild noises outside their one-room cabins—scratching in the dirt, rustles on the roof, thunder-cracks in the woods, moaning

in the wind—Christian settlers could repeat the words of
Genesis like a mantra, trying to drown out the din of the
unfamiliar: "And God blessed them and God said unto
them, be fruitful and multiply, and replenish the earth and
subdue it." Shored up by a sense of duty and privilege, the
settler plans fences, calculates acres to be cleared. A
sudden fury of winter wind through a crack in the wall
extinguishes the candle flame. He closes the Bible and
listens in the dark as snow pounds against the cabin and
the walls groan and snap in the cold. Will the roof hold
up under all the snow? Should he light the lantern? Put
more wood on the fire? A sound like a rifle blast cracks
the air, and his heart pounds. It's just the cold exploding
the sap in the trees by his cabin. Will the snow barricade
his door? For how long? Will he run out of wood, freeze
in here with the wood just inches away outside? How thin
and desperate those biblical commands sound in this
place.

But thousands of years of opposing the wilderness can't
be wiped out by a few months confronted by a contradic-
tion: the chaotic riot of weeds and wild animals that the
new settlers build fences to keep out feeds the indigenous
people and supplies them with a livelihood while the
settlers starve for want of cultivated crops. My ancestors
did not see this lush place as a paradise. It was savage—
beautiful, but frightening—and the settlers fortified themselves to battle it, to build a Garden of Eden, surround it
with walls, and fill it up with as many familiar things from
home as they could get their hands on.

The walled cities of early civilization birthed the Judeo-Christian myth that locates paradise inside a walled garden. In *Beyond Geography,* Frederick Turner explains, "What was within the walls, within the reaches of the irrigation ditches, was nature subdued, controlled, put to proper use; what was beyond, whether land, people, or spirits, was savage, unpredictable, malevolent." In Canada, what stands between the settler and wild nature are only the walls of the log cabin. The dread of what lies beyond the walls is most evident in the settler women's stories. Amelia Harris, the daughter of a Loyalist, describes her mother's constant fear for her little boy in the wilderness of Upper Canada: "[I]f He was out of her sight a few minuets [*sic*] endless misfortunes might befall him. He might be eaten up by wild beasts or He might be stolen by the Indians, their stealing children not being a very uncommon occurrence in those days, and during the Summer Season there used to be Hundreds encamped on the Beach, or he might be drowned, or He might wander away and be lost in the woods. . . ."

In *Roughing It in the Bush,* Susanna Moodie, who settled a bit later, describes a night she spent alone in her cabin, waiting for her husband to return: "The night had closed in cold and foggy, and I could no longer distinguish any object at more than a few yards from the door. Bringing in as much wood as I thought would last me for several hours, I closed the door. . . . Hour after hour wore away, and the crowing of the cocks proclaimed midnight, and yet they came not. I had burnt out all my wood, and

46 A PILGRIM IN IRELAND

I dared not open the door to fetch in more. The candle was expiring in the socket, and I had not courage to go up in the loft and procure another before it finally went out. . . . Just as the day broke my friends the wolves set up a parting benediction so loud and wild, and near the house, that I was afraid lest they should break through the frail window, or come down the low, wide chimney, and rob me of my child."

In my mother's papers was a letter from my great-aunt Kate. Her mother, my great-grandmother, was born in Canada in 1856, a few years after her parents fled the potato famine in Ireland. Aunt Kate told my mother the story of her older sister Maggie, the eighth child in the family. "Maggie was your Dad's little sister. She died before I was born. She had scarlet fever and got swollen up after being outside on the damp ground. She got kidney blockage and those days the Drs. didn't have the med. to treat those things. I remember my Mother holding up her thumb and saying she had black curls this long all over her head. Poor Mother when she found out she was pregnant again she cried, and Lizzie who worked for her, said Maybe this baby will be a comfort to you in your old age. I hope I was."

Driving through Southern Ontario, I recognized that the taming of chaotic nature had continued, even in the twenty-odd years I'd been away. The dark places that stirred me with electric fear as a child were just the neglected corners of the world I lived in, corners that no one had had time yet to tidy up and civilize. We can't seem to stop ourselves from "improving" the landscape around us. It's our Judeo-Christian prime directive. Even the wild places we preserve, like provincial parks, we feel compelled to mow and spray with pesticides and equip with hot showers and flush toilets.

Carl Jung writes: "As scientific understanding has grown, so our world has become dehumanized. Man feels himself isolated in the cosmos, because he is no longer involved in nature. . . . No voices now speak to man from stones, plants, and animals, nor does he speak to them believing they can hear. His contact with nature has gone, and with it has gone the profound emotional energy that this symbolic connection supplied." But the fear that drives us to improve nature, like Susanna Moodie's mounting paranoia in her bush cabin, is a kind of paradox. We wouldn't fear the dark wild places if we didn't sense that something lived there, something we can't understand, even with our twenty-first-century scientific knowledge. And I think that those European women who had moved into the Canadian bush, though they vehemently denied it, lived far closer to the voices that speak from stones and trees than we do now. Catharine Parr Traill finds herself "disappointed in the forest trees" because of their "want of picturesque beauty." But in the ragged unfamiliarity of the Canadian wilderness, she feels the profound emotional energy that Jung talks about, and she has the good sense to fear it: "We soon lost sight entirely of the river, and struck into the deep solitude of the forest, where not a sound disturbed the almost awful stillness that reigned around us."

How long does it take for the unknown to become the known, for the nightmare fear of the bone-chilling wolf cry to become a song that lopes through your dreams on a moonlit night? For Catharine Parr Traill, a couple of years in the backwoods of Canada, getting to know the forest and its wildflowers, was enough to make her briefly speculate that "some years hence the timbers that are now burned up will be regretted." And in *Loyalist Narratives*, Susan Burnham Greeley writes wistfully: "And what a grand and solemn sound proceeded from those glorious woods when the wind blew hard. It was not so considered then, it sounded so like the rush of great waters that it was thought to come from the Upper Lakes and was generally spoken of as 'The Lake is roaring, there will be a storm.' But the Lakes are here, though the forest is not and the grand music of the woods is heard no more."

AWAY

Wherever it may lead, the perilous journey is always, of course, perilous. In Celtic folktales, [the hero] often risks bodily harm, even death, as he quests for a marvellous object that he believes will bring luck, health, or a richer life. . . . Every quest story is an initiation in which the hero learns, in varying degrees of success, the answer to the age-old question, "Who am I?"

—TOM COWAN, *FIRE IN THE HEAD*

FLYING INTO SHANNON AIRPORT in County Clare felt like travelling backwards in time. And not just because Ireland is a country where people remember 1649 as if it was last week, or because they still burn peat to keep their homes warm. It's because my ancestors were formed here, formed over time as much as the pitted and creased limestone that covers the northern part of the county. Like a geologist trying to understand the formation of the earth, I was going backwards to what I thought was the beginning, to try to understand the formation of me.

My quest in Ireland was not an original one; thousands come here every year, the curious great- and great-great-grandchildren of the millions of Irish who have been scattered to the four directions. Like thousands of others, I've come to clamber over sun-warmed tombstones, searching for names grown over with cream white roses gone wild among the stinging nettle, egocentrically asking, "Is this where I came from? Is this part of me?"

From the window of the hostel, the morning looked clear: super-bright blue sky, a deeper blue than home, with a navy tinge to it; super-bright, almost white sun; and only a few clouds. But when I stepped outside, a brisk, cold wind picked up the flaps of my jacket. I shivered and bent to tighten my boot laces.

I had made my way to Doolin, County Clare, on the edge of the Burren, to meet the land that two of my great-great-grandmothers had left behind. On my map, I had highlighted a semi-circular path around the top half of Ireland, to cover most of the counties my family had come from. Clare was special. As little as I knew about these two women, I knew more about them than I did about almost any of the other grandparents in that generation.

My great-great-grandmother Rose Convey lived in County Clare as a child. She probably left Ireland around age thirteen or fourteen and travelled with her family first to Baltimore, just before the worst of the potato famine hit. She later married my great-great-grandfather Owen

Leonard, a man from Northern Ireland, settled in Warkworth, Ontario, and had eight children. Anne Quinlivan was born in the town of Ennis, probably around the same time as Rose, about 1830. Her life followed a similar path. Some time in the 1840s, she immigrated with her family to Upper Canada, where she met Hugh Dillon, from Cushendall, Northern Ireland. She had twelve children over a period of about twenty years. By the time she gave birth to her last child, in 1872, she had seen two of her children die, one four and one ten. I figured out these ages of death myself, but then I saw that my mother had already pencilled them in lightly on a chart. Anne's last child, Charles, died when he was only eight days old. Anne followed him three days later, probably as a result of complications from childbirth. Margaret Ann, my great-grandmother, would have just turned four when her mother died.

I have a newspaper clipping from 1973 reproducing a very old photo of another set of grandparents from that same generation. Great-great-grandma Mary Smith has her hands clasped for the photo. Her hair is parted in the middle and drawn back, her brow is deeply furrowed, her mouth a tight line of worry. Probably dressed in their best for the picture, the family wears dark, modest, and worn clothes. When I think of these women's lives, I imagine them as difficult and often sad. When one child died, the anxiety for the others would dog them the rest of their days, a constant uneasy watchfulness. They might wake up in the middle of the night, panicked to realize they had relaxed into an unguarded sleep, then listen to hear the distinctive breathing of each child. When they thought of Ireland, was it with longing for home and peace? Or did the hardships of the famine years make them shudder to think what their lives would have been like if they had stayed behind?

When I left Ontario and moved to Winnipeg, I was just a bit younger than Rose and Anne were when they immigrated to North America. Our family had taken the train, and we watched the hills around Lake Superior and the rocky Canadian Shield gradually fall away until it seemed as if we were left with nothing but an expanse of pale yellow fields pierced occasionally by a chunky grain elevator, then the backstreets and warehouses of the city. Being in a city was completely foreign to me. I remember feeling like a corralled horse, itching to get free and run in an open space. I couldn't believe my parents had chosen this over our farm in Ontario. I climbed into the papery-smelling crawlspace in our house on Sharp Boulevard, listened to the noises of kids playing on the sidewalk below, and longed for the smells of skunk cabbage and elderberry.

In County Clare, I planned to walk the places where my great-great-grandmothers might have walked. My pilgrimage here was partly to meet this physical geography. I knew that in Ireland, geography and spirituality were, and still are, often intertwined. A spring is a shrine, a mountain forms a pilgrim's challenge, a hill is a home to the people of the Otherworld. I had the idea that if I touched the same rocks, felt the same wind on my face, sat on the same dirt as my ancestors, the land would whisper something so subtle and simple it would slip past the neat categories my mind had waiting for it and I would just understand. But I had told my family I would be doing "research," and I worried about their expectations. I felt the weight of my family papers tucked in the pocket of my backpack, insisting that this pilgrimage was not just for me, but also for them, for my mother, even for Rose and Anne and the others who had never come home. Would my half-cocked "research" be enough to bring back something worthwhile? Or something at least worth the RRSP I had spent to get here?

EVEN AFTER ALL THE READING I'd done, a stubborn image of Ireland persisted somewhere in my imagination: a place peopled by children as carefree as fairies with damp curls and dirt-smudged faces, and old people with sharp tongues, tweed caps, and twinkling blue eyes. They would all be named Paidraig or Maire, and they would never have set foot out of the villages where they were born. The city people would be tough and fiercely political, given to bursts of song and fist fights.

The Irish have been saddled with both romantic and despicable stereotypes. In nineteenth-century British and North American cartoons, the Irish are portrayed as dirty, lazy, drunk, immoral, savage, and illogical. They are often drawn with ape-like facial features to suggest that they are lower on the evolutionary scale. An editorial in the London *Times* during the famine years looked forward to "an era when a native Irishman would be 'as rare on the banks of the Liffey [in Dublin] as a red man on the banks of the Manhattan [*sic*]'" In the mid-century flood of immigrants to America, employers would often put up signs reading, "Help wanted. No Irish need apply." The stereotypes, though, have slowly mutated into more positive ones, the kind that I am stuck on.

Karl, the hostel warden at the Aille River Hostel in Doolin, was the first Irish person I spent time talking to, and I quickly realized how insulting it was that I expected his country and culture to have remained frozen in some kind of Old World authenticity. He was a down-to-earth but cosmopolitan musician of about thirty, with a fashionably unshaven face, a hoop earring in one ear, and a backwards baseball cap pulled over his ponytail. He had the soft Irish brogue, but it wasn't as pronounced as the local accent. He was educated and widely travelled. In fact, I was surprised to learn he had taught on a reserve in northern British Columbia for a year, and he was curious about the similarities between the aboriginal hand drum and the Irish bodhran. I got the feeling that in northern B.C., Karl had been struck by something familiar and beckoning too. Talking to Karl gave me an unsettling awareness that if my heritage was here, it wasn't waiting to embrace me as I got off the plane.

First-time travellers to Ireland seem to have a hard time getting their heads around the place. On the surface, the quaint little villages seem to be from another time, with their peat bricks in the fire and fences made of stone and traditional music in the pubs, the bodhran tapping at our hearts to remember. And we think we do remember. We think this mysterious place is part of our past, and we want to discount anything that doesn't fit. In another fishing village on the west coast, I went to a tiny pub one night with an Irish student and a young German woman from the hostel where I was staying. The pub owner lived upstairs, and the pub itself was just a few tables squeezed into the corner of his kitchen. If you wanted to use the bathroom, you had to go upstairs to his private quarters. Most of the people around the table were regulars who liked to chat with the hostel staff and the tourists who passed through.

After introductions, the German woman said to one man, "You're a fisherman?"

His face flushed with annoyance, but he composed himself and said coolly, "I'm a meteorologist."

An embarrassed silence fell over the table. A meteorologist licking stout foam from his lips in a bar in a seaside village doesn't fit. But the Irish have no trouble with paradox, and they seem to grow a little weary with the tourists' wide-eyed wonder. In another part of Ireland, I one day joined a young American who wanted to stop in at O'Sullivan's pub because her name was Sullivan. We went up to the bar to order our pints.

"Are you O'Sullivan?" she asked.

The bartender nodded.

"My name is Sullivan!" she said. "I'm from America."

The bartender frowned. "What are you having?" he said tersely.

The American was offended. I felt for her. She had thought she might have stumbled upon a distant relative. But I felt for the bartender too. It's hard to put your finger on what's offensive about it—the foreigner breezing in, trying to claim a piece of your history, what you've lived and never thought fit to desert. And here I was, a little more discreet than Ms. Sullivan but sniffing around just the same for the scent of something pure that I could put in a bottle and label "My culture."

I suppose I was expecting some kind of welcome in Ireland, maybe a shock of familiarity. Maybe that was why the homesickness swept in on me so soon. In this case, home was a person. It was the first time I'd travelled alone since I'd met David. Before I met him, I'd travelled alone in places like Morocco and Mexico and Guatemala. But in this place, where I spoke the language, knew how to use the pay phones, and had the comfort of hot running water, loneliness appeared like a blister my first time out in new boots. My tight budget had squeezed me into close proximity with other people, and ironically, that made the loneliness swell up. I don't mind spartan accommodations; I even pride myself on being able to get comfortable in the chill of a Sahara December in a dank four-dollar-a-night hotel room in old Marrakech, with a candle for heat and cold water only in the courtyard shower. In Mexico, I slept happily in a hammock suspended above the sand, with thin bamboo walls separating me from the crash of the ocean surf. In Portugal, I stayed as a guest in a house where all night the shadows of rats criss-crossed the bamboo ceiling above me. As long as I have the luxury of being able to close some kind of door on the world outside, I can get used to most anything. But dormitory rooms—bunk beds full of strange night-time sighs and coughs and the tossing bodies of strangers—they give my body bedbug twitches and keep my mind reeling noisily all night. I wake up, if I've slept at all, from a peaceless night's sleep and am forced to start my day by smiling at some long-legged German stranger who's dangling his hiking-booted feet over the edge of his bunk and brushing his teeth for fifteen non-stop minutes.

That first night in the hostel in Doolin, the travellers, chock full of Guinness, started to stumble in in the dark. One climbed into the bunk above me. A few minutes later, someone else came tripping through and climbed into the same bunk above me. I was nervous. I didn't know how strong the bed frame was. I lay in my bunk without moving, my blanket tucked up under my chin, and stared at the slats of the mattress support above me. The two of them rustled around in their polyester sleeping bag, whispering in that loud hiss that's worse than normal volume. I was just considering suggesting that one of them should sleep on the floor—which, having weighed the possibilities of appearing to be an unromantic prig against the reality of being crushed by inaction, both literally and figuratively, seemed to me to be a fair compromise—when someone else stumbled in heavily, apologizing drunkenly. He climbed into the bunk above me too.

The first two took a long time to notice that someone else was in their tiny bed. I waited. Any normal person would swing her legs up bicycle-style and pummel the mattress with her heels till someone fell out. The homesick person lies paralyzed, torn between hysterical laughter and hysterical tears, waiting for the three of them to come crashing down.

When they finally figured out that there were three of them, they were exceedingly polite about it. They worked out some kind of arrangement; in the dark, it was hard to tell what. Curses and apologies flew around the dormitory for about ten minutes as they settled themselves. I lay awake till dawn, my mind and body rushing with the delirium tremens of too much social interaction. What was I doing here with a bunch of Guinness-sampling tourists anyway? Didn't I have some sort of legitimate claim to County Clare? Didn't my blood run through here?

The next day I told my sorry tale to Karl and begged him for a private room. He made a pot of tea, sat by the turf fire with me as we drank it, and asked me about my husband's origins. About the private room, he said, "I'll see what I can do." Later that afternoon, he showed me to a small, bare room under the eaves of the house, with a futon on the floor. I spread my books and pens out on the floor beside the bed with a shudder of pleasure and swung open the window to let in the Doolin wind and sunshine.

I LEANED ON THE BOTTOM HALF of the farmhouse-turned-hostel door and watched a bright yellow rescue helicopter cast its shadow over the navy and green Irish landscape as it chopped its way towards the black cliffs edging the ocean.

"Another tourist too close to the cliff edge," said Karl. "There's a couple go over every year."

The night before, a German woman had told me about watching another woman drop off the rocks to her death on other cliffs, not far from here, on Skellig Michael. Tour guides said it was the first accident of its kind in a thousand years of pilgrims. But Karl laughed at that.

"The first?" he guffawed.

"Is it dangerous?" I asked Karl.

"'Tis. If you go too close to the edge. And if the weather's bad. The sea comes crashing up against the rocks. It can sweep you off the rock, all right, before anybody notices you were even standing there."

"Hmm. Maybe I'll take the road," I said.

"You have to take the footpath," he said firmly. "You don't see anything from the road." And he went inside to stoke the peat fire.

Even though the morning was sunny, and I'd been there only a couple of days, I knew enough not to trust the clear sky. It could change in a matter of minutes. I packed my rain cape and took the high road that led out of town towards the footpath to the Cliffs of Moher.

The walk to the cliffs was to be my first acquaintance with the forbidding Atlantic coast of Clare. Cecil Woodham-Smith writes that on the west coast of Ireland, the famine distress was "most severe." I had often

wondered why the Irish didn't save themselves by eating
fish, since the Atlantic Ocean was spread out before them,
teeming with herring and mackerel, and in deeper water,
cod, ling, sole, turbot, and haddock. I wasn't the only one.
English officials who visited Clare in the 1840s puzzled
over the problem as well. James Hack Tuke found that
nets and tackle had been "pawned or sold 'to buy a little
[corn] meal,'" a move that, for some, reinforced the idea
that the Irish were imprudent and lazy. But as Woodham-
Smith explains, by the nineteenth century, timber for boat-
building was almost non-existent on the west coast. The
Irish built instead light curraghs made of wicker and
covered with hides. They were fast and efficient on the
Atlantic swells but could not handle the heavy nets needed
for deep-sea fishing. And the sea crashing into the cliffs
made the waters close to home treacherous.

My *Lonely Planet* guidebook had a little sub-heading
under the Cliffs of Moher titled "A Risky Route." The
path I was taking would cross an area known as the Cliff
of the Colts, apparently because some fairy horses went
galloping over the cliffs and crashed into the Atlantic
below. I told myself this was a good initiation into the
Clare landscape, a solo journey tinged with an element of
danger. When I came to the end of the gravel road, I had
to slip through a steel livestock gate and trudge through
mud and manure past three farmers who were gathered
around a tractor. Like other footpaths I would take in
Ireland, this one kept tricking me into thinking I had gone
the wrong way.

"Is this the way to the cliffs?" I asked, sure I was trespassing on their property.

They all nodded. They'd been asked this question many times before.

"Just keep going. You can't miss it." And that was a phrase I'd hear many times again, knowing that I could and, with my infallibly mistaken sense of direction, probably would.

Up ahead, a herd of cattle grazed across the path. I walked slowly, watching for bulls. When they saw me coming, the cattle galloped away on stiff legs. Breathing in gulps of thick, humid air, I climbed the path steadily till I was at the crest of a hill that looked down across the sloping green fields, the village of Doolin and its pier, and southwest to the rugged black cliffs and stretch of ocean.

Then I was over the crest of the hill and utterly alone. The muddy rock-and-bog-studded hills rolled out empty all around me and away. I could hear the waves crashing against the rocks below. The surf gushed into gouges cut out of the land. I stopped every few minutes to scan ahead for the path, and my step became less certain as I tried to distinguish between cow and human prints in the mud. I didn't want to get myself too close to that cliff edge and not be able to get back up.

A couple of planks were laid across a trickle of tide in a gouge, and I knew I was still on the right path. I scrambled down a few more gouges, across wet rocks, and up again. I was exhilarated, knowing I couldn't really go wrong as long as I kept some distance between myself and that edge that looked as if it had been recently bitten out of the green fields by a giant mouth.

Then I saw the mist, grey and rolling in from the ocean in waves, sweeping across the land up ahead and engulfing it. I'd been reading Yeats, stories about "the gentry," fairies who live in the Otherworld and can be glimpsed just at times like this, when the world is "betwixt and between"—near water or bog, in mist and twilight, neither this nor that: the Celtic twilight. They come rushing from beneath the Hollow Hills and fairy forts to mix with humans, and sometimes to toy with them. I remembered that writer Tom Cowan says sometimes people stumble into the world of the fairies by taking a false step on a well-worn path or on "stray sod." I froze in my steps. It was all stray sod to me, far from the sod I knew.

At these haunted times, when the doorway is open between chaos and order, the gentry may take a human to come and live in the Otherworld with them. The Otherworld, according to those who've been there (and many have, though they don't all like to talk about it), is occupied by the little people, the ancestors, and other stray spirits. The taken human's body remains in this world, going through the motions of everyday life as if in a dream, or sometimes taking to bed or becoming reclusive and unable to take part in this world at all. Every night for a few hours, she travels to the fairy forts, lit up by tiny lights, alive with lovely music and dancing and extravagant feasting. The taken one may be forced to work for the fairies or become their lover or bear their children. Sometimes she will be mistreated, but usually she will be given some benefit in return, like an extraordinary success with crops in our world, or some unusual cleverness or strength.

For seven years at a time, she is "away," just a husk of a body, uninhabited by the essence of what makes her human. After seven years, the opportunity comes to return to the world again. When the taken one comes back, she doesn't know any time has passed at all. I couldn't help wondering what would happen to a foreigner who was taken "away." Would the body be able to get back home? Seven years. David would be long gone when I got back to Regina.

The mist billowed in about a hundred feet in front of me, moving fast. Without one of my amulets from home at hand, I picked up a stone from the path in front of me and rubbed it. "Please don't let this mist engulf me," I said aloud. As the mist swept towards me, I prayed faster, but it was too late. I felt the soft damp brushing my face. It wasn't rain, but it was thick enough that I could see the tiny droplets hanging in the air in front of me. What little path I had been clinging to disappeared, and it disappeared behind me too and I couldn't see six feet in any direction. My heart did a clean dive into thick panic. The primordial soup of fog swirled around me. I could hear the cotton-batting-buffered slosh of the sea, but where exactly was it coming from? As I stood frozen, listening, I thought it might be coming from the rush of my own blood.

I might have stayed in this expanse of bog and mud and grass, found a rock to perch on and wait out the mist safely, without worrying about a false step too close to the invisible cliff edge. But it had come along so swiftly and turned the day so quickly to twilight that it felt as if the place was permanently changed. I thought it might stay enshrouded in the thick grey cloud, tinged with the green of the landscape, that wasn't quite rain, and the only thing to do was walk out of it.

Strangely, the cover of mist began to overtake my panic with an unreasonably soothing calm. The edges were gone. Gouges to fall into were gone. The village behind me, the tourist attraction a few miles ahead of me, everything I had been worrying about was gone. Maybe I should have been suspicious of that, known that the fairies were near and I was glimpsing a world where the buzz of human activity, worry, work, planning, and failing were meaningless, where seven years passed in an hour and an hour spun out to seven years.

I watched my feet step one in front of the other, and I held onto my stone as the sea sound surged against cliff. I started singing, quietly at first and then louder, the eagle song I'd learned in British Columbia, my cracking, disembodied voice floating up out of the swirling mist, a pitiful little human thing asserting itself in the void. If I had ancestors lurking in the foggy Otherworld, surely they would see how hopelessly foreign I was, singing songs attached to another land altogether.

It must have been more than an hour that passed,

because somehow I had covered the ground that was supposed to take two hours. A hiking-boot-clad couple walked towards me, and I clamped my mouth shut, embarrassed by the volume of my singing. Things began to take shape around me—a road; a parking lot; tour buses; grim, disappointed tourists hung round the neck with cameras; and stalls draped with T-shirts and Aran sweaters and postcards.

"There's nothing to see," the couple told me. "Just fog."

I made my way to the coffee shop, still holding tight to my stone. I ordered a pot of tea and a piece of apple tart with cream and sat by a window to wait. I was absorbed in the last bit of crust and cream when I looked up and saw the mist rolling away, sweeping across the parking lot as fast as it had come, leaving super-blue sky, confident yellow-white sunshine, and the jagged, wet black Cliffs of Moher I had come to see.

LATER THAT EVENING, I walked out to the Doolin pier to watch the sunset. Lines of cloud had gathered out over the Atlantic in purples and oranges. Yeats collected his stories of Irish folklore in the late nineteenth and early twentieth centuries. He tells hundreds of stories that were recounted to him by Irish people, especially in the west of Ireland, about instances of being "away." No conflict seemed to exist between the "pagan" nature of the stories and the fact that the Irish had been Catholic for several centuries. So I wondered, when the Irish emigrated, what happened to their belief in the parallel, underground world of spirits and fairies? Did the new immigrants think they had left the fairy forts and all of that behind in Ireland?

If they got close enough to the aboriginal people around them in North America, they would hear echoes of the old Celtic beliefs, maybe unnerving echoes, given how far they'd travelled. Around them lived people who accepted as completely normal the presence of spirits in the land, rocks, and trees. On a walk in the woods, they might come across pieces of cloth tied on the bushes around a spring, just as some Irish did with their springs and wells at home. They would learn that certain spots should be avoided for building a house or pitching a camp because they were the paths of the ancestor spirits. If you slept on the path of the spirits, you'd feel the feet of the old ones knocking up against you all night long, trying to get by. In Ireland, too, people knew to avoid the paths of the "others." Aboriginal medicine men and women, if they met them, would remind the settlers of people like the famous Irish wise woman Biddy Early, who lived in County Clare around the famine years of the nineteenth century, and who found cures in the plants and could travel between this world and the Otherworld. Just as in Ireland, many of the aboriginal medicine people had fallen gravely ill at some point in their lives and been at the edge of death, and when they returned, they became apprentices to a spiritual craft that set them apart from the everyday world.

Like Biddy Early and other Irish wise men and women, the aboriginal medicine people were at the least an embarrassment to the Church. To discourage people's stubbornly persistent belief in their power to heal, the Church called them witch doctors, savages, and heathens. Priests literally dragged the Indians from their ceremonies and threatened them with abuse, temporal and otherwise. I wonder if a huge, soul-racking sense of relief shuddered through the Irish Catholics when they saw that, this time, they were not the targets of punishing restrictions on their faith. Spirits and little people and fairy forts? Maybe they did exist in the new land. But best to keep your mouth shut, init?

THE BURREN

*Men who lived in a world where anything might flow and change,
and become any other thing. . . . had imaginative passions because
they did not live within our own straight limits and were nearer to
ancient chaos, every man's desire, and had immortal models about
them.*

—W. B. YEATS, *WRITINGS ON IRISH FOLKLORE, LEGEND AND MYTH*

THE WIND ON THE WEST COAST of Ireland reminds me
of the Canadian prairie wind, that starts up, summer or
winter, and blows for days on end. It sings through the
timbers of your house, and in the night, it smacks dead
branches and debris up against the side of your dreams.
Wailing hounds you from your REM sleep, and you listen,
worried about toppled trees, snapped power lines, broken
windows, downed aircraft. And that human moan you
think you hear, the low-pitched one, could it be a cat, the

neighbours' baby, what? If you're waiting for this wind to
die down, you could be waiting a long time.

In the hostel in County Clare, I lingered by the turf fire
in the morning, fortifying myself with strong tea and
buttery biscuits, and hoping for the wind to relent. A
hardy young woman with a friendly fuzz of white-blonde
hair, rosy cheeks, and effervescent blue eyes came in,
breathless with the wind. She had a warm, delighted laugh
and a pair of sturdy hiking boots. She introduced herself
as Denise, from the former East Germany. She was
recently separated from her husband and travelling alone
for the first time. When she heard that I was travelling
without my husband, she didn't raise her eyebrows.
Instead, she leaned closer and took out a map of the
Burren. I took out mine. Behind the liveliness of her eyes,
I discovered, was a soft melancholy that made her pensive
and companionable. We decided to walk the "green road"
through the Burren together.

The Boireann, which means rocky place in Irish, is a
large region of limestone in County Clare. It is filled with
the ruins of ancient sites, like tombs, forts, churches,
castles, and cottages, some thousands of years old, some
more recent. It seems hard to imagine anyone scratching a
potato patch into the rock, but the Burren was once home
to large numbers of Irish, as evidenced by all the ruins left
behind. In 1841, when my great-great-grandmothers were
children in Clare, a census shows the Irish population
stood at 8,175,124, making this the most densely popu-
lated country in Europe, according to Woodham-Smith.

And County Clare's population, it was discovered, had been underestimated by one-third. The dense population meant that no corner of land would be ignored, even land coated in as thin a layer of soil as the Burren. Rose and Anne could have lived on the Burren. Or they might have visited this part of the county. At the least, they would have known the place as a strange landscape where strange things happened.

If it wasn't for Denise's enthusiasm, I might have waited by the fire, listening for a lull in the wind. But instead I bought a warm wool cap and put on three layers of clothes: a cotton shirt, a wool sweater, and a Value Village reversible raincoat. We set out, each armed with detailed maps that almost, but didn't quite, cover the area we were crossing. We planned to walk north, up to Formoyle Chapel, then along the Caher River and down to Fanore, a distance of about twelve miles, where we'd catch a bus or a lift back.

You wouldn't think you'd need a map, till you get out there. Some of the "green roads" are overgrown make-work projects from the famine years, when the British saw fit to make the lazy, starving Irish earn their charity by building useless roads. Others are hundreds of years older than that. They've been turned into an ingenious system of walking paths that criss-cross the scenic loneliness of Ireland. Many are unsignposted, except for, sometimes, a little green sign, courtesy of the Irish tourist board, at the start (or end?). They peter out into muddy trails through patches of woods, sometimes lead to someone's farm or nowhere, sometimes curve abruptly and run into another green road that looks unnervingly the same, especially on the Burren.

But Denise's and my partial maps noted ring forts and ruins and dolmens, and we were walking too eagerly to have any doubts about where we were going. We were each armed with a tourist's sense of purpose. Denise, a botanist, wanted to see the quirky mix of plant species on the Burren. I wanted to see the stone vestiges of a history that spanned the pre-Celtic, pre-Christian, and pre-famine times. The tantalizing details on T. D. Robinson's Burren map suggested that the mysteries of the past were written in the landscape. I hoped I would find clues to my own past here.

The wind spun our hair into haloes around our sensible hats. Our noses and eyes ran with water. My boots rubbed against bandaged blisters from the day before. We walked four miles before we reached the start of our trail. I worried that I might have misrepresented myself as a serious hiker.

We left the main road and ducked under a fence onto a well-beaten, grassy, stone-packed path that was more than a path but not quite a road. For a mile or two, we walked confidently, leaning into the wind. Then we crested a small hill and saw the Burren. It stopped us. I felt as if I'd happened across an arrowhead in the dirt at a city bus stop. My sense of order tilted.

The bizarre, still landscape of pitted grey limestone rolled out before us like a hidden test site recovering from

secret chemical experiments. The folded hills were giant
caved-in rock soufflés appearing, then disappearing. Stone
was everywhere: stone in piles, stone in lines, stone in
circles, stacked stone, random stone, heaved stone. But it
was not only stone. It was spotted with the deepest green,
sometimes in smooth, sweeping sheets, and sometimes,
like a bad shave with a dull razor, in sparse little tufts
between stones. The green was sprinkled with tiny
flowers—purple, hot pink, yellow, white. Above it all was
the Irish sky, as big as a prairie sky, but moody and otherworldly, a tweed of deep blues, then puffs of dryer-lint
grey clouds, pulled thin by wind and threatening rain. The
old grey hills, speckled with fingerprints of thousands of
years of humans, swam around me as troubling as a
dream whose archetypes created no echoes of recognition.

The Jungian psychologist Aniela Jaffé sees stones as one
of the most enduring religious symbols in human history.
From ancient times, stones were thought to be dwelling
places of deities or spirits. T. W. Rolleston, writing in
1911 about the myths and legends of the Celts, says that
stones, along with rivers, trees, and mountains, were
"objects of veneration." Holed stones were believed to
hold healing power. In 452 A.D., the Synod of Arles
denounced those who venerated trees, wells, and stones.
But the recognition of the sacred nature of some stones
persisted among the people. In Stó:lō territory, where
David's reserve is, certain stones are believed to have once
been people, until the XeXà:ls, the transformers, came
and altered them. These stones still possess spirit.

I looked at Denise, and she giggled with delight.

"See these flowers?" she asked. "These are Arctic and Alpine and Mediterranean. Yeah, all mixed together! You see because there's the sea and the wind and the rock." She squatted and took a tiny purple flower gently between her fingers.

Stone ruins crusted with turmeric yellow lichen rose from the earth. This one could be a shelter put together last year by a farmer for his cattle. Or it could be the remains of a thousand-year-old castle. Some of the structures were made of stacked stones that fitted into each other so closely we knew they'd been shaped by centuries of wind and water. Large ones as big as coffins made up the foundation, then flat ones were stacked on that, with long small ones stuffed in the cracks like newspaper in a log-cabin wall.

When we studied our maps, it was hard to tell if the skinny line referred to that little path up there, which was hardly a path, or if the ruins indicated by a thin circle on the map could be this pile of stone that looked something like a fence. We stood on a cratered moon, trying to get our bearings.

Denise said, "Oh! I see a ring fort!"

"Where?"

"There. Do you see that bump there? And those rocks?"

"I think I see it. . . . You mean that curving part?"

"No, just to the right. There."

So as not to appear obtuse, I murmured vaguely. It all looked like lines of rock to me, and except for the obvious

walls, I couldn't tell what had been built by human hands
and what had been tossed into odd accidental shapes by
nature.

When a dolmen heaved diagonally into view, though, it
was unmistakable. A giant stone slab was perched on two
other giant stones to form a chamber about twice the size
of a refrigerator. Part of it had sunk into the earth over the
five thousand or so years it had been there, so that it
seemed like an appendage growing from the limestone.

Tom Cowan says dolmens are pre-Celtic tombs,
"mysteriously vacant doorways" that lead to the
Otherworld. Celtic shamans saw them as portals to
another world too, and they crawled inside to visit with
the ancestral spirits. Even Christian monks felt themselves
closer to the sacred inside them. I thought about dropping
to my stomach on the pitted rock and worming through
the blank mouth of stone myself, a *circa* Y2K secular
adding my name to the list of seekers after the sacred. But
it wasn't the kind of thing you did with the flippancy of
posing for a photo while planting an upside-down kiss on
the Blarney stone. I was stopped by fear. If it really was a
doorway, could you cross back to this world at will? And
if the Otherworld was one specific to this land alone,
could I get lost in there, a stranger twice removed? I imagined the wind singing through the cracks in the stone, the
echoes of the world outside, above, below, reverberating
between the stone sides of the chamber. The spirit of the
land would speak in there, all right, if you knew how to
listen. If you didn't go mad first.

Out here, the wind seemed like the only living thing.
My hair was a tangle of it, and my ears roared with it until
I had to clap my hands over them just for a moment's
peace. But the landscape stayed strangely still. There were
no leaves to dance in whirlwinds. No trees to bend. Just
these implacable stones and the tiny wildflowers poking
stiffly through cracks in the limestone.

The Gaelic word for wind is *sidhe*. *Sidhe* is also the
name for the fairies who people these rocks and hills and
rove on the wind in bands. Christianity has done its best
to banish the *sidhe* from Ireland, but on the Burren, the
wind is a chorus of their keening, whispering, pleading,
and singing. I could see how the Irish would perceive an
invisible host of mischievous, sometimes wicked, beings
occupying the constantly shifting realm of the wind. I
tried to imagine spending a week out here, helpless against
the relentless hammering at what I know as real.

Yeats cautions that too much curiosity about the *sidhe*
will lead to a loss of interest in things human. Curiosity is
the first step down the slippery slope to the underground
fairy world, which is recklessly happy—out-of-control,
relentlessly gay, both irresistible and sinister. Sinister, he
says, because a life without sorrow is unnatural to
humans. Some humans are only "touched" by the *sidhe,*
spun into a dream state but left among the living to act as
servants for the little people.

The little people live in Canada too. I first heard
about them at an exhibition of Allen Sapp paintings.
Sapp is a world-renowned Cree artist who paints almost

supernaturally realistic paintings of life on his Saskatchewan reserve. I was looking at some paintings of the sun dance when Delores, a Cree friend, asked me if I'd noticed the tiny little figures in some of Sapp's images. I had, but I thought they were supposed to be normal-sized people, portrayed from an odd perspective for some artistic reason. Delores said they were the little people. Some traditions believe the little people are the keepers of the sun dance, or of healing knowledge. On the East Coast of Canada, they are known, like the fairies, to appear to humans near places that are "betwixt and between," neither water nor land: lakeshores, marshes, riverbanks, and creeksides. Like the Irish fairies, aboriginal little people have a reputation for playing tricks on humans, especially those who are foolishly sure of themselves. They have also been known to steal people, especially children. Tracie Williames, a Shuswap woman who was interviewed in 1964, remembers her grandmother's stories of the "wee tiny people that came from the bottom of the rocks . . . a tunnel in the mountain. She forbid us to go near these holes, said it was dangerous. . . . She said there was wee people that come out of there and they were very dangerous. They'd steal the Indians. They'd put up a horrible fight."

In the mid-nineteenth century, in his book *History of the Ojebway Indians,* the Ojibwa reverend Peter Jones, born Kahkewaquonaby, wrote about the fairies around Lake Ontario, where my Clare ancestors migrated: "The heathen Indians all believe in the existence of those imaginary little folks called *Fairies*. The Ojebways call them *Mamagwasewug*, the hidden or covered beings. They believe them to be invisible, but possessed of the power of showing themselves. Many old Indians affirm that they have both seen and talked with them. They say that they are about two or three feet high, walk erect, and have the human form, but that their faces are covered over with short hair." Jones explains that they love red cloth and prints, and that leaving pieces of the cloth near their haunts is a guarantee of good luck. He relates the story of a Scots family in 1824 whose home was visited by "some strange invisible agencies." Jones asked a noted chief what he thought of the strange occurrences among the whites. He answered that he knew all about it. The place where the white man's house was built was once the residence of the *Mamagwasewug.* "'When the white man came and pitched his wigwam on the spot where they lived, they removed back to the poplar grove, where they have been living for several years. Last spring this white man went and cleared and burnt this grove, and the fairies have again been obliged to remove; their patience and forbearance were now exhausted. . . .'"

Across Ireland, farmers' fields are dotted with fairy "raths," conspicuous mounds often covered with bushes and left untilled to avoid disrupting the little people's homes. In Northern Ireland, I asked a middle-aged woman for directions to a "fairy rath" I'd heard about.

"Have you heard of it?" I asked.

"Aye. The children set the fairy bushes ablaze at Hallowe'en."

"Can I walk to it?"

"You can, o' course," she said. "It's straight on. But you don't believe in that, do you?"

I laughed a bit and didn't answer. But that she asked at all gave me the impression that she was trying hard to wash her modern mind of an old belief. Probably most of the farmers that steer clear of the fairy forts would deny believing in them. To outsiders, leprechauns have mostly become a kind of childish joke, green cardboard cut-outs pasted on school blackboards on St. Patrick's Day. But everywhere, old beliefs die hard. I don't believe that a disembodied white-haired god in the clouds can see into my mind and know my sinful thoughts. But just to be on the safe side, I cut a wide swath around that dark place myself.

It's easy enough to accept, intellectually, that capricious little beings could make up part of a people's belief system. What's harder to understand is that these little people are not just quaint pieces of folklore, good for trotting out at cultural festivals or for fashioning into garden ornaments. People really see these beings. And in places as far apart as the Burren in the west of Ireland and Saskatchewan in the west of Canada. It seems that often it's children who see them. Usually, you just catch them out of the corner of your eye. Sometimes they are dressed all in yellow; other times they have faces like tree bark. One young woman told me about the coulee on her reserve in Saskatchewan; people leave plates of fish, Wayne Gretzky hockey cards, and other gifts for the little people who are known to live in that spot. It's said that if you're not afraid of them, they can help you.

Antoine Lonesinger, a Cree man from Saskatchewan who was interviewed in 1974, tells a story about a man named Bare Belly. One day in 1918, Bare Belly was walking home from another reserve when he became confused by the wind. He missed the road and became completely lost. "He was standing on a hill listening and trying to get his bearings, when he heard what he thought were children talking and laughing. The voices were coming towards him and he waited. Then someone said, 'Grandpa, give us some tobacco and we will show you the road to your place.' He gave them tobacco and they led him a short ways to the road. 'Here is the road. You just follow it and you will get home,' they told him. 'But before you go, here is a present for you,' one of them said, as he placed five little stones in Bare Belly's hand. These stones were flat and round and very smooth, and all had a little hole through them. Bare Belly found his way home that night, and never became lost again."

Not everybody believes the little people exist, but for those who have seen them, they're very much alive and well, living lives parallel to ours in a realm we can't see. And it is the land that offers openings into their world. Aboriginal Canadians, like the Irish, have long memories attached to the land.

A few years ago, I visited a friend who was living for a

summer at Nimpo Lake, in the Chilcotin area of British Columbia, doing baking for a fly-in fishing camp. The float plane would fly in every once in a while to pick up her fresh bread and supplies and fly them out to the camp. Since she couldn't leave the lodge, she introduced me to Fred, who was planning to go out in the bush to scout out sites of pine mushrooms. Fred was an expatriate American about thirty years my senior. He had been a logger in Oregon when logging was still done with saws and axes. In the sixties, the first time he ever left home, he came up to that remote part of Canada, felt good there, and stayed. He was a soft-spoken man whose ability to maintain an amiable silence when he had nothing to say would be called shy by those of us who lived with the constant hum of human chatter. He lived alone by a secluded lake in a well-built one-room cabin heated by a woodstove made from an oil barrel, with no electricity and no running water. He made his living hauling trees, chopping wood, and pursuing whatever other bush enterprises came along.

Fred and I gathered a few camping things and packed them into his well-worn early model Ford Bronco: some tea bags, potatoes, a jar of home-canned salmon, candles, an axe, some bedding, and a tarp. Fred liked to travel light. We had that in common. We headed west on the road to Bella Coola, a gravel road that cuts straight and wide through the crackly, dry Jack pine forests of the Chilcotin Plateau, then pitches down a skinny, dizzying 18 per cent grade along the side of a canyon and into the lush rainforest of the coast. This is a road that was chopped through the canyon in the fifties by Bella Coola locals itching to get out once in a while. In some places, it was just wide enough for one car. If you had the guts to look over the precipice and into the canyon, you could see the history of automobiles, rusting out in the sun. Fred pumped his mushy brakes madly on the descent as the burning tires barely held on in the gravel.

That night we camped. To the east of the mud logging road was a mess of recent clear-cutting: torn stumps, ragged strips of bark, and bulldozed piles of forest debris. To the west was an old-growth pine forest. Under the huge trees was a soft, thick blanket of moss and almost nothing else. I had never seen such a clean forest floor.

"I feel pretty good about this place," Fred said.

With the tarp, we set up a lean-to big enough for two strangers to sleep under. We made a small cooking fire on the road, so as not to start an underground fire in the moss. When we put the fire out, the night was deep, dark, and still. The slightest wind sighed through the pines and some old trees creaked gently. I fell asleep and awoke to see the moon was up and the straight bodies of pine trees were quietly watching me.

Early in the morning, as Fred slept, I went looking for a creek to wash in. I found a swath of clear-cut that was growing in with bright purple fireweed and salmon-berries, wet with dew. I walked along a slippery dead log, eating berries as I went. The quiet was thick and heavy, like a soft substance I was moving through. I had the feeling I was being watched. When I looked down the clear-cut, I saw a bear calmly scooping berries into her snout, ignoring me.

That day, not far from Bella Coola, Fred and I went looking for some aboriginal petroglyphs I'd heard about. Fred thought he knew the place. We scrambled along a slippery creek bank into a rainforest thick with cedars, ferns, and mushrooms and smelling of sweet, musky rain, mud, and leaves. With practised balance, Fred measured out a fallen cedar at twenty-five paces. Somehow in the crush of vegetation, he found the petroglyphs: several large, flat rocks overlooking the creek, baked by steamy sunshine and etched with enigmatic drawings. If I was going to carve a poem into stone, I would pick a place like this.

I spent only about an hour there, but I'm still haunted by it, by something I perceived only at the edges and couldn't explain. If I spent even a year, if my blood ran for generations through the same place, I think I would begin to perceive what exists beyond the edges, maybe even to see the little people traipsing merrily along the cusp of everyday reality.

IT WAS PROBABLY MY FAULT that Denise and I got lost on the Burren. I say that because usually when I travel, I take elaborate care to note landmarks, coming and going, since at least half the time I'll walk into a building, come out, and head confidently in the exact wrong direction. I have such a reliably dysfunctional sense of direction that

I've learned that if I'm absolutely sure that east is on my right, I'll go left, knowing I'm certainly wrong. I have ended up hopelessly lost in the labyrinths of tiny European streets and in Moroccan souks, trying to smile nonchalantly as I pass the same stall of leather purses for the fourth time. On the Trans-Canada Highway, I've been alarmed to awaken from driving a stretch of prairie highway when I suddenly register the same landmarks I passed before I stopped at the gas station. I have learned not to deviate spontaneously from my planned course. But when I'm with someone else, I relax my guard, count on the probability that most people are better navigators than I am.

We stopped to have lunch in the shelter of a ruin that might have been a castle wall or might have been a small barn. The rock walls were hewn by weather into comfortable age, and there was no roof. We took out our Irish soda bread, cheese, and oranges, and Denise spread her plastic rain cape on the grass. The sun almost came out; it almost rained. But the wind still poured through the gaps in the walls. We were quiet, because to talk we had to shout over the ringing in our ears. After we ate, we stretched and took some photos, and then, to warm up my blood, I ran back up to the path.

Denise took some more photos, then joined me, and we began to walk. I remember I looked back at our lunch shelter and felt disoriented. Nothing looked the same as it had when we had stopped. I couldn't locate the place where we'd left the path to cut across to the barn-castle. I noticed two paths joining in a V that I hadn't noticed before. Denise, when I glanced at her, was smiling and tilting her face happily into the wind as she walked. So I ignored my disorientation, since "dis" can really apply only to someone who is oriented in the first place.

I don't know how far we walked before we started to notice the landscape changing. We had reached a fork in the road heading into a cultivated conifer forest. Above us, the sky was blank grey, sunless. We consulted Denise's map and found nothing we could recognize.

"This is not right," Denise said. "May I see your map?"

It, too, had nothing in common with the land we were looking at.

"There should not be a forest," Denise said.

"There's a forest on this map," I said. "But it's way over here."

"Yes. We should not be there. I am thinking we were about here. Could this be this road?"

"I wonder if we might have taken the wrong path after lunch," I suggested casually.

"There was only one path," Denise said.

Could we have gone in one side and come out the other? With no shadows to guide us, with the wind clawing at us from every direction, could we have set ourselves down on a new road walking south instead of north? Maybe the little people hijacked our human plans, picked up and spun the ruins while we ate, and dropped us down, like Dorothy in Oz, on a far corner of the Burren.

We decided to take the road that seemed to be heading back to the coast. That way, we reasoned, we would eventually find Fanore. But even that didn't make sense. According to our maps, the Sitka spruce forest we were heading into lay east, not west. We walked on, sheltered from the wind now. The green road rapidly deteriorated into chunks of rock and mud. It seemed that we might be on an old creek bed. Denise whistled little songs and I made jokes. The path looped into circles, then disappeared into guesses.

Before us lay crest after crest of rolling, empty hills. The horizon was buried in a pale green that was neither cloud nor land. No sun, no sea to orient us. The edges of our maps were blank, and I had only a skewed sense of the scale we were looking at. It was a long way back the way we came, but striking out across the unmarked hills with no idea of the direction we were heading wasn't a plan we considered. We were subdued as we retraced our path. We'd been walking several hours in the cold wind, and we were getting tired.

We emerged into the village of Fanore disoriented, like someone who has awakened to find that the stranger knocking at the door in her dream was really the roof shingles coming undone in the wind—the real blended with the unreal so that we weren't sure where one ended and the other began.

Denise and I heaved ourselves onto stools in the dark, quiet village pub and ordered pots of hot tea to which we added lots of sugar. Some weathered old men smiled and nodded, and when they spoke, we couldn't understand a word. Outside there was still a soft grey daylight and a bus was due to arrive, more or less according to schedule. We smiled to ourselves as we sipped our tea. I had a camera full of photos and the strange feeling that when I developed the film, it would all be blank.

St. Brigid's Well

*Sometimes I feel like a motherless child
a long way from home.*

— Traditional Song

On a warm day in county clare, I walked up the
highway from the Cliffs of Moher, looking for St. Brigid's
Holy Well. My guidebook called this a pre-Christian site,
a sacred spring where people went for healing and for
their prayers to be answered by Brigid, the Mother
Goddess. A deity of fire, wisdom, poetry, and home, she is
a triple goddess, with sister deities of healing and
smithing. In the pagan tradition, her celebration day is
February 1, Imbolc. This date was adopted as the saint's

feast day when converted pagans refused to abandon the various Brigid springs around Ireland and Catholics instead christened them St. Brigid's Holy Wells. The stories of the goddess Brigid and the saint Brigid have become mingled into an appealing Celtic-Christian mythology about a powerful, compassionate woman, prayed to as the guardian of agriculture, midwives, and healers. I met another Catholic woman traveller who had visited some of the other St. Brigid's wells that still exist in Ireland. Brigid had an allure for those of us disillusioned Catholic women who felt that our spirituality should be grounded in a place, in the physical world we lived in. We also relished the fact that the Irish loved Brigid the goddess so much that they wouldn't give her up.

I'd been told that the well was "straight on," I "couldn't miss it." Maybe I was expecting big signs, big crowds, tour buses. But I managed to miss it. I flagged down a car, and they drove me to the edge of Liscannor. I'd come too far. A motorhome full of elderly French tourists stopped and took me back up the road a stretch, and then I saw it: an unassuming statue and cross shaded by a grove of trees.

I sat on a stone bench in the garden area behind the spring, calmed by a palpable peace in the tender breeze rustling the trees and vines, the birds singing, the leaves making shadow patterns on the stones. A woman who had been whitewashing the entrance to the spring was quietly putting away her tools. No one else was around. From the pocket of my knapsack, I pulled a deep red, pearly plastic rosary out of a tangle of gum wrappers, loose change, lint, and hair elastics. My grandmother, whose two grandmothers both came from County Clare, owned this rosary. When she died, my mother kept it. Both of them would have disapproved of the way I normally kept it in a drawer twisted among other chains and earrings I never wore. Both of them would have loved this place, among the birds with the sound of trickling spring water. St. Brigid would have been a saint for them; they probably knew her.

Brigid, born around 450, apparently received many offers of marriage. In the Irish life of Brigid, as recounted in *Celtic Spirituality*, we are told that a promising suitor came to her father's door, much to the excitement of her father and brothers. However, Brigid told him, "It is difficult for me, since I have offered up my virginity to God." Instead, she recommended a beautiful girl who lived nearby. Her brothers, who saw themselves being deprived of a healthy dowry, became angry and told her, "The beautiful eye in your head will be betrothed to a man whether you like it or not." Brigid poked her finger into her eye and pulled it out, saying, "Here is that beautiful eye for you. I think it unlikely that anyone will ask you for the hand of a blind girl."

Shortly after, Brigid took the veil. The Irish life of Brigid claims that the bishop was so intoxicated with the grace of God in Brigid's presence that he "did not know what he was reciting from his book, for he consecrated Brigid with the orders of a bishop." She is credited with numerous miracles: finding lost cows, healing lepers and cripples, and even helping a pregnant girl who had taken a vow of chastity by relieving her of her fetus "without birth or pain." One well-known miracle tells how she came inside, dripping wet from a fierce rainstorm. Some rays of sun broke suddenly through the cracks in the walls, and she absent-mindedly hung her wet clothes on a sunbeam, mistaking it for a beam of wood. The clothes stayed there, hanging on the fragile ray. News of the miracle spread. Brigid eventually founded two monasteries, one for men and one for women. She also founded a school of art, known for metalwork and illumination.

My mother and grandmother would have approved of Brigid's spirited defiance. She was always "up and doing," just like the energetic women they themselves were. Well into her seventies, Grandma raced around the Niagara Peninsula in her little green Comet, teaching, taking painting classes, working on Catholic Women's League projects. My mother's independence took another tack, but it was in the same spirit. She told me that Grandma had wanted her to be a nun. Why not? Grandma's sister was a nun. One of her brother's daughters, Mother's cousin Ellen, became a nun, and she was an energetic thinker like Brigid, unafraid to make waves in the Catholic establishment. After high school, Mother took business classes at a Toronto convent school operated by the Sisters of St. Joseph, but she told me she had no taste for the nuns' controlled kind of life. If she was going to be single, she would live her life in a cabin by a lake, doing oil paintings for money, something she had a talent for.

She married relatively late, patiently waiting for a man who would make it worth doing. My dad remembers frequent drives home from Toronto with my mother and grandmother not long after they met. Grandma sat in the back seat and said the rosary the whole trip, a habit that drove my father crazy. The fact that he patiently held his comments must have been one of the things Mother appreciated about him. She also told us she loved nail polish before she met my father. She had about twenty bottles of it, and she carefully painted her nails to coordinate with her outfit of the day. But when she found out he didn't like painted nails, she threw every last bottle into the garbage barrel. I can't even imagine my mother caught up in such a dramatic gesture.

Until meeting my father, she worked as a bookkeeper and travelled with her girlfriends to places like New York, Chicago, and Montreal, and to the cottage country around Huntsville. She also made pilgrimages to shrines in Michigan, Wisconsin, and Quebec. Her drawers were full of prayer cards from these shrines, as well as little booklets of novenas to the saints and details of apparitions. If she had found the opportunity to come to Ireland, I know she would have sat beside this same quiet spring that honoured St. Brigid. But she never travelled overseas to see the famous shrines that rang in her imagination, places like Lourdes and, especially, Fátima.

I AM FORTY YEARS OLD, and my mother has been dead for almost fifteen years. But I think that when I am seventy, I will still feel like a motherless child. Sometimes I'm startled by the familiar smell of her face powder and the tangy cosmetic perfume of her trademark Revlon honeybee pink lipstick, and I try to hold the scent close, as if she has just left the room. Ghosts live in the sounds that were her sounds and the smells that were her smells: hiss of hot iron on spray-starched cotton; snip of scissors giving home haircuts; melodies hummed off-key; plunk of potato bugs landing in empty soup cans as we made our way along the rows of potato plants; snap of her purse clasp; scent of Wrigley's spearmint gum and Chanel No. 5 on linty, lipstick-stained Kleenexes. When I hear the solid clack of a woman's pumps on a parquet floor, I don't turn to look, but I slow down and wait for the ghost of her hand taking mine.

My mother had eyes in the back of her head. She knew what the six of us kids were doing at all times, she said. If you grow up in the Catholic Church, that kind of magic doesn't seem far-fetched at all. I wanted to believe it. I also wanted to believe, when my brother and I took refuge from a thunderstorm in the hammock under the kitchen window, that lightning could turn out to be not lightning at all, but a messenger from heaven, telling us we'd been specially chosen, like the three shepherd children in Fátima, Portugal. I wanted an apparition of the Virgin Mary to appear to me while I was catching turtles in my grandparents' pond, and for people to come from all over the world, walking on their knees and crutches up Pelham Road to be healed by the magic Smith pond water. I took special pride in having the same name as St. Francis of Assisi. I wanted the owl that came around my bedroom window at night to whisper prophecies through the screen. I expected that at any moment, something miraculous would happen to me and I would be ready for it.

My mother was an extremely practical woman who could spear bats with a pitchfork, drive a tractor, or tear a strip off a lippy sales clerk. But her faith ran mysterious and absolute. She was not interested in questioning the stories we heard at Mass every Sunday. My father went to church, but his religion seemed to find more expression in the classical music, usually Mozart, he listened to every Sunday at high volume. My mother turned the volume down, and gradually it crept back up. He conducted imaginary orchestras from the cigar-smoke cloud encircling his chair, and he read: books about evolution, the human as animal, and the workings of the mind. Occasionally, over bacon and eggs after Mass, my father poked fun at the priest's human slant on the divine. My mother tolerated it with a cryptic smile that suggested those little loops of logic were trivial nonsense she had no time for. Her faith, something intimate and private and not to be analyzed, operated at a much deeper level.

The story of the three shepherd children of Fátima resonated in my mother's Catholic heart like the tinkling of an altar boy's handbells. She told us about the illiterate Lucia and her little cousins, who were out herding their sheep on the thirteenth of May, 1917, when the wind suddenly calmed, the sky dimmed, and a brilliant flash of lightning heralded the beautiful apparition of the Virgin Mary. Hovering above a small oak sapling, Mary told the children to wait for her on the thirteenth of every month for six months, after which she would reveal to them what they must do. News leaked out about the apparition, and a crowd began to gather with the children the day before the thirteenth of each month, until, by some accounts, about one hundred thousand people converged on the site on the thirteenth of October.

Not everybody believed the children. Some people, who were trying to usher in a new, forward-thinking, anti-monarchist, anti-religious era in Portugal, were embarrassed by this supernatural hocus-pocus. They sputtered indignantly at the mention of miracles carried by clouds and other meteorological phenomena. In newspaper editorials, they pounced on inaccuracies; parades and demonstrations trailed through villages, mocking the Catholics' ridiculous faith. An anti-Catholic mayor even kidnapped the children on the thirteenth of one month to prevent them from going to the clearing at the appointed time. Like children who are not quite confident they've outgrown Santa Claus, the modern-minded, including some priests, threw themselves zealously into trying to destroy the Fátima magic.

But on the thirteenth of October, 1917, all the people gathered at the site saw the same thing: a lustrous mother-of-pearl disc of sun whirling wildly in the sky above the little oak tree where the children had seen the apparition. Everything was bathed in purple then yellow light, and at

times, the sun dipped towards earth, as if about to drop
from the sky. The crowd watched this for about ten
minutes, then fell to their knees in the mud.

In response to the miracle, the Freemasons published a
contemptuous reaction addressed "to All Liberal
Portuguese":

*[T]he sun, at a certain hour on 13th October, 1917 . . .
in the height of the 20th century was seen to dance a
fandango in the clouds! This, citizens, is a miserable and
retrograde attempt to plunge the Portuguese people
once more into the dense darkness of past times which
have departed never to return. The republic and those
citizens who are charged with the noble and thankless
task of guiding it in the glorious paths of Civilisation
and Progress cannot consent to the degradation of the
people into fanaticism and credulity. . . . What shall be
the means of co-operation with those from whom we
claim the action necessary for the end we envisage? An
intensive and tenacious propaganda, which will raise
the mentality of our co-citizens to the realms of Truth,
Reason and Science, convincing them that nothing can
alter the laws of nature and that pretended miracles are
nothing but miserable tricks. . . . Let us then liberate
ourselves and cleanse our minds, not only from foolish
beliefs in such gross and laughable tricks as Fátima but
more especially from any credence in the supernatural
and a pretended* Deus Omnipotente.

But appeals to reason and science had the same effect on the faithful as your family's disapproval of your boyfriend. The relationship turns even more intimate, secret, and sacred for your being the only one privileged enough to see his virtues. Martyrdom appeals to a lot of Catholics, and the controversy about Fátima only served to whip their faith into a frenzy of certainty.

As a kid, I loved the story of Fátima almost as much as my mother did, and any stories of the saints, who were just regular folks seeing and doing miraculous, magical things. I could be next. My sisters and I had our little paper *Lives of the Saints* books, and we liked reading about how each of them had achieved his or her fame. The saint we were each named after was supposed to be our role model, our inspiration for how to lead a life that paved the way for miracles. I had several St. Franceses I could choose as role models. There was St. Frances Xavier Cabrini, an American saint, the patron saint of immigrants. As a young woman, she abandoned her early dream of being a missionary in China and went instead to New York to work among Italian immigrants. She spent her life travelling through America, Europe, and Central and South America, founding orphanages, schools, and clinics. Frances of Rome, the patron saint of motorists, was a fourteenth-century saint with a tragic story. Though she longed to become a nun, her family forced her to marry. Her husband was imprisoned for his religious affiliations (which seemed handy to me—unwanted husband out of the way!), her first-born son was kidnapped, and their home and property were looted, then confiscated. Later, her other two children died. In the face of all of this, Frances founded the Oblates of Mary, a group of women committed to caring for the poor and sick. She was tormented by visions of temptation and claimed to be protected from them by a guardian angel who stayed steadfastly by her side. I'm not sure how this translated into being the protector of motorists.

My favourite saint Francis, though, was actually a man, the famous St. Francis of Assisi. For one thing, he was well known enough to be included in even the slimmest *Lives of the Saints,* which made me one up on my sister, whose namesake, St. Barbara, was discredited in the 1960s. But his story was also the most romantic of the Franceses. As a young man, he lived a life of ease and privilege with his cloth merchant father's money in twelfth-century Assisi. He spent his days partying, singing, and reciting poetry with a crowd of young followers. One day when he was praying, he heard a voice telling him to "go and repair my church." Starting with the obvious message in the command, he stole cloth from his father's shop, sold it, and used the money to repair the town's crumbling churches. When his father complained, Francis renounced his wealth in a dramatic gesture: he stripped himself down to nothing in Assisi's market square and handed the clothes back to his father. This symbolic act set him on a path of poverty, a pared-down life travelling the country-side, preaching. He soon attracted companions who wanted to live their lives in the open air, following the example of the disciples from the Gospel. But what St. Francis is most famous for is his conviction that all of nature was part of his brotherhood. He preached to wolves and birds, and the stories say that the animals listened to him.

"My" saint did become a model for me. When I was fifteen and living on our farm east of Winnipeg, I carried a miniature Bible my sister had given me for my confirmation as I hauled water and shovelled manure. I sat on straw bales in the barn and read the Bible to my cows, which I'd named Ecclesiastes, Luke, Ezekiel, and Joshua. I lived always in the shadow of St. Francis's dream: that the most honourable life I could lead would be to renounce all my possessions and live in the woods, minus the preaching part, unburdened by material things.

FÁTIMA EXEMPLIFIED MY MOTHER'S FAITH. The charge that believing in such miracles was irrational would have annoyed her, I think, since she saw herself as what she was: practical, energetic, and resourceful. And the miracles did have an extremely practical aspect to them: you prayed for help with your life—illness, financial problems, marriage difficulties—and sometimes you got it. But more than anything, I think it would have puzzled her. What do logic and reason have to do with faith anyway? Her brand of devotion to beliefs that flew in the face of all rational explanation came to be what I most loved and most hated about the Catholic religion.

My mother had the Irish love for faith torture tests.

These were meant to be not public displays, but personal
stamina tests, like those of the pilgrims at Fátima, who
walked for miles on their bloodied knees to the shrine of
the Virgin Mary. Or like the pilgrims at Croagh Patrick
in Ireland, who made a 2,500-foot climb up the mountain in bare feet, praying all the way. One New Year's
Day in Winnipeg, Mother wound us into mummies of
wool and oversized fur coats and herded the whole
family to Mass a mile away, on foot, through a forty-
below blizzard. Later, when we moved out to the country
east of Winnipeg, the prairie extremes offered many more
opportunities for daredevil acts of death-defying faith.
My mother commandeered my sister's innocent city
boyfriend one blizzardy Christmas Eve to chauffeur all of
us, in his ageing Chevy Belair that needed a wheel alignment, to the Polish Catholic church half an hour away.

The mile roads around there slice poker straight
through the bland, bald prairie. When the snowfall is
heavy, everything looks the same: a wide flat expanse of
soft, dangerous white; snow coming at the windshield in
dizzying meteor showers. Where the road is is anyone's
guess. You feel your way along, blazing skinny tracks
through the thick snow, adjusting the steering wheel back
and forth madly to stay on the road. The ditches are more
like riverbeds, wide and deep, and when you hit them
going forty miles an hour, the car sails and lands with a
soft, surreal poof, then sickening silence.

The Polish Catholic church was a small wooden-sided
box of a church, with no detectable heating system, lit

by fluorescent lights under the stained-glass windows and the soft glow of votive candles from the front. The Polish priest's accent was so thick it sounded like he'd popped a handful of marbles in his mouth before Mass. We couldn't understand a word he said. To my mother, it was clear, what he said wasn't that important. The man doing the reading from the Gospel according to Mark—"The voice of one crying in the wilderness, prepare ye the way of the Lord, make his paths straight"—paused to make an announcement: "There's a car in the parking lot with the lights on." Hearts bottomed out like mufflers at a washboard crossing. Mental checks in the trunk for booster cables. I imagined looking down from the sky like God, the sad faltering headlights making dimming circles in the fury of snow in a postage-stamp parking lot, a pathetic little patch of human fallibility in the over-whelming expanse of the prairie. "It's a blue station wagon," he added. Necks craned, looking for the unlucky owner who'd have to face the dull groan of a frozen igni-tion on the coldest night of the year.

If I ever missed a Sunday Mass, it was because I'd gone on Saturday night or was deathly ill. Those were the only two good reasons my mother could see for skipping Mass. But I was sixteen and couldn't see the point of shivering in a little shack of a church, muttering singsong prayers from rote while the wind hurled spitballs of snow against the stained glass and the snow threatened to form an impenetrable plug in the church driveway. We could be at home by the woodstove, drinking hot chocolate and eating bacon-and-tomato sandwiches, thinking spiritual thoughts.

On summer Sunday mornings, I dragged myself to Mass fighting hangovers in the choke of parking-lot dust and stifling hot, garlic-laden air. Saturday nights, I parked the pickup truck at an abandoned gravel pit, wedged in next to souped-up Beaumonts and Cougars with their doors open and Boston blaring from the eight-track. My friends and I, and other teenagers from miles around, had been drawn to this pit on this night, instead of one of the several other possible pits where no one would be, as if by a giant magnet of teenage desires: to escape the soul-destroying good intentions of our careful parents, who tried to get us to join them in the living room and talk about our day; to cast off Nancy Drew and stuffed animals, forty-fives of John Denver and the Partridge Family, and all those things that held us to our childhood. We wanted to immerse ourselves in ear-bleeding AC/DC, guzzle Canadian Club and Coke or lemon gin and 7UP, smoke mudweed, grind our hips into the bony blue-jeaned hips of boys we never saw at school. We slid down gravel banks in our wide-legged pastel-coloured Wranglers; later, we'd try to figure out how to explain the mud stains to our mothers. We proved our invincibility by diving blindly into the dark water of the pits. I tried hard to convince myself that nobody had their eyes in the back of my head.

Every weekend I came in half an hour or so past my one o'clock curfew, with a stick of Dentyne in my mouth to mask the alcohol on my breath, and went to my mother's side of the bed to kiss her goodnight. She was always awake, waiting for me, but she never once asked me if I'd been drinking. People I knew bar-hopped the country motor inns, then got on their snowmobiles and drove them into the sides of trains, invisible black bulks snaking along through wheat-stubbled fields. Some rolled their cars and drowned in the deep ditch water. Ugly jealousies erupted over girlfriends or money, and teenagers shot each other or themselves with their dads' shotguns. One night, some of the CN crew dropped acid, then got in an axe fight on my friend's porch. We toked from the water pipe or hot knives till we couldn't speak, then got in our cars and drove home. I was seventeen, eighteen, and thought my mother's naïveté ran deep and wide. Now I realize she knew a lot more than I thought she did. She kept quiet, and I believe some nights, listening for the whistle of the pickup coming down the gravel road and the crunch of tires in the driveway, she must have prayed.

AT EIGHTEEN, I MOVED to the anonymity and freedom of Winnipeg. I had a $165-a-month apartment on an elm-lined street in St. Boniface, a French-Catholic part of the city. My apartment was an appendage of a large house made into suites. Tucked away near the back lane, it had its own entrance, through a tall gate. I felt like no one knew I was back there. I passed the Catholic church on the corner of my street every day; summer nights, I sometimes walked to the cathedral and sat on the steps, watching the stars twinkling on the river. I saw the northern lights dancing over the trees there one night. But I didn't go to Mass.

Sunday mornings I slept in. My bedroom walls were painted pale lilac and the windows were placed high on the wall. I opened them to the smells of summer and the sound of feet crunching gravel in the back lane once in a while. I kicked off my sheets and lay there in the soft light, listening to church bells ringing and feeling a delirious rush of freedom.

I wrote long letters about religion to my father, who I saw as my ally in doubt. He had gone to Mass faithfully every Sunday of our young lives, but as we grew up and my sisters left home, he'd found excuses to miss some Sundays. He told me about his own parents' secret: while his mother took my dad (an only child) to Mass every week, his father pretended to opt to go at a different time. When he grew up, my dad discovered that instead of going to church, his father actually walked downtown to a restaurant, had coffee and a piece of pie, and read for an hour.

By the time I got to university a few years later, my mother had stopped asking me when I'd last been to church. By the time I arrived out at the farm on Sundays for a visit, my mother had already changed out of her church clothes and into a cotton blouse and walking shorts. I helped her in the garden or made gravy for the roast beef while we chatted about plants or my new apartment or my younger brother. We didn't talk about religion.

I didn't tell her that I had become friends with a poet, and that we stayed up drinking tea in the Lithium Café or the Blue Note Café all night or until they kicked us out, then we walked home over the bridges to St. Boniface in the mauve dawn. I didn't tell her that I had fallen in love with the existentialists, those grey-faced philosophers who were overwhelmed by the bland nothingness of a pair of purple suspenders. In the humid Winnipeg summer mornings, I loved Nietzsche for approving of my desire to "live dangerously! . . . live at war with [my] peers and [myself]!" or Sartre for confirming my suspicion that "man is nothing else but that which he makes of himself." Intoxicated with the encouragement to make my own morality, I was casting off Catholicism like my sisters' hand-me-downs now that I had my own spending money. Faith like what I thought my mother had seemed to me to be a security blanket that would prevent me from living my life with courage and the strength of my convictions. I was tired of walking around with the unshakeable feeling that someone had his eye to the peephole of my soul.

But my definitive break with the Catholic Church came later. I was in my second year of university and living with my boyfriend, the nicest guy I'd ever met, polite, kind, and fun too. I wasn't the first of my sisters to live with a man "in sin." My oldest sister, Anne, had bravely blazed a trail of broken rules right through her teenage years in the sixties; in fact, all my sisters but one had lived or were still living with men. So my mother had had time to get used to the idea. She didn't like it when they did it, and she didn't like it any better when I did it, but she didn't say much about it. She wasn't the kind of mother to bang her head against the wall, or rail against the danger we were putting ourselves in. Anyway, everything she could have said I knew, and she knew I knew. But still, I felt a constant invisible pressure to legitimize things. I think it was me who suggested we get married. I was only twenty-two and about to break the rule I'd made for myself never to marry before thirty.

To get married in the Catholic Church, Steve, a non-practising Protestant, and I had to do some marriage preparation classes. Part of that included meeting with an old white-haired priest who seemed a little bored with the whole process. Our meetings took place early in the morning, out at the University of Manitoba. I never ate breakfast and it was a long bus ride out there, so by the time we were in the meeting, I was feeling weak with hunger. At our last meeting before the wedding, the old priest was rattling off questions and nodding absently at the answers when he suddenly became very serious. He leaned towards us, saying, "Do you understand that marriage is forever?" At that moment, the bookshelves, the big oak desk, and the priest's serious eyes all began to swim in front of me like a thick soup being stirred. I stood up slowly and clutched the desk as he waited for my answer. Then I lurched towards the door in hopes of making it to fresh air, but it was too late. When I vomited, the door caught most of it; the rest hit the floor. Steve jumped up and steadied me, helping me down the hall to the bathroom. As I rinsed my mouth and splashed cold water on my face, I heard the nuns in the hall wheeling out the bucket to clean up. I imagined they thought I was pregnant. In retrospect, Jung would probably say my unconscious was telling me I couldn't stomach the idea of "forever."

It took only two years of marriage for us to realize how young we really were. I think it was my idea to get divorced too. In the back of my mind, I thought it would mean the ultimate split with the Church, since I knew that this refusal to accept the human institution of divorce was one of the things that set the Catholics apart from other Christians. If I divorced and married again, I would be committing adultery. I could not receive Communion ever again, but I could, according to the catechism of the Catholic Church, stay with the Church and spend the rest of my days making myself truly sorry for being the sinner I was. I could see that I had boxed myself in, religiously speaking. If I had continued to live with Steve in a state of sin, I could heartily repent for it and go on being a full-fledged Catholic. But because I'd taken a half-hearted stab at trying to live by the Church's rules and failed, it was game over.

I NEVER UNDERSTOOD my mother's spirituality. Even now I understand only that it went deeper for her than I imagined. In my mind, faith served as a cautious invest-ment. You wanted to stay in the black. You made bargains when you prayed: "God, if you'll only give me this one

thing, I promise I'll start going to church. . . . If you'll only
give me this one thing, I won't ask for anything else for at
least a whole year. . . ." When bad things happened, I felt
that I was being punished, and I'd rack my brain for what
I'd done that was offensive. I didn't think of only God
watching me; all my dead relatives jostled for a peek
through the peephole of my soul when they had the time
for a minor sinner like me. I learned this kind of religion
from my mother, but I must have missed a big chunk too,
because by my system, what good could it do you if it
didn't keep you in the black? What good could it do you
if bad things started to pile up on you and the prayers
didn't help a bit? What good could it do you if it couldn't
save you when you needed it most?

In 1986, I caught the train from Conçeição, a fishing
village in the Algarve, to Lisbon. From there, I took a bus
to Fátima. A couple of months earlier, my mother had
discovered that the bumps on the back of her neck weren't
strange, persistent insect bites, but lymphoma. She had
just turned fifty-nine, was otherwise healthy, and still
worked full time. Shortly before the diagnosis, she had
given up caffeine and taken up daily swimming to try to
improve her waning energy level. But by then the cancer,
like some malevolent spirit, had already found an opening
and moved in to possess her. Her original plan had been
to meet me in Portugal, not only because she thought the
healing power of Fátima might be stronger in person, but
also because she was seized by a furious burst of desire to
do all the things she hadn't yet got around to doing. But

while she was waiting for just the right moment between chemo sessions, my mother's health worsened and she asked me to make the pilgrimage for her.

A hard rain had been hammering down for days, but it had stopped by the time I got off the bus in the town of Fátima. Four-star pale peach concrete hotels dominated the main street; I found a room in a dim, hushed little pension run by nuns. By coincidence, the day before had been October 13, the anniversary of the apparitions. Most of the crowds had cleared out already, leaving the little town empty and slightly dishevelled. Dripping trees surrounded the entrance to the site. Inside, a huge, bare stretch of pavement glistening with rainwater sprawled like several mall parking lots strung together. A few straggling pilgrims on their knees dotted the pavement, known as the Way of Penance. It was like a rock concert after the bands have packed up. It seemed an unlikely place for miracles.

At one end of the Way of Penance, a large basilica wrapped a semicircle of arched, columned stone around the site. At the bottom of the basilica's steps I saw a more inviting spot, the Capelhina, the little chapel that Mary told the three shepherd children to have built in her honour. I knelt on the steps of the open-air chapel, trying to pray, feeling cynical and annoyed at the Church, which had originally been so reluctant to accept the three children's apparition story and now seemed to be cashing in on their irrepressible popularity. But as I watched the knots of pilgrims picking their way through puddles, a panic of faith clutched me suddenly, the same mysterious surrender to the unreasonable that had appealed to me as a child. I looked up, past the clay-tiled roof of the chapel, and saw a bright double rainbow arcing across the rain-washed sky. Like the shepherd children, I took it as a sign. Then the clutch of hope that had wound itself so tightly around my heart let go like a spring ricocheting danger-ously inside me, and I bent my head and cried for all the things my mother deserved.

I'm Catholic enough to accept a rainbow as a sign of a benevolent God, but not enough to accept divine plans that override my own. So I didn't accept it gracefully when, a few months later, in spite of the faith she main-tained stubbornly, my mother was buried with the rosary I'd bought for her in Fátima.

BACK AT ST. BRIGID'S WELL in County Clare, I went around and out of the sunlight into the dim, narrow passage to the spring. The whitewashed stucco entrance and the cement platform built around the spring looked so ordinary and unspectacular that I felt ready to be disap-pointed by another tacky tourist attraction. As my eyes adjusted to the shadows, I saw that the platform had been painted forest green with a blood red cross on it. A thin green moss clung to the old stone of the well. Bright red waxy flowers and vibrant English ivy dripped across the sunlight above a piece of corrugated metal. The mildew-encrusted area around the well was crowded with offer-ings left by pilgrims: vases of faded silk flowers, statues draped with rosaries, old curled photographs and new ones, notes, little pieces of clothing. Pieces of red cloth were tied to the lush branches overhanging the spring. But what knocked me off my intellectually curious high ground was one child's running shoe, placed right in the centre of the little platform above the water.

Like a blow to the back of the knees, the sincerity of generations of prayers overwhelmed me—mothers with sick children, husbands with wives dying in the famine, people whose loved ones were missing or were slipping away from cholera, influenza, fever. At this spring, they knelt on the damp stone and prayed for help from a woman as sturdy as the women who loved them. In the dim, cool shade by the spring, they might feel comforted like I did by a simple, motherly calm, like a strong, warm hand that cups the back of your neck.

I left the rosary there, for my mother and for my grandmother. I hung it from a branch with the others that were there, with the spring water trickling quietly over stones, the way it had for more than a thousand years.

I know that forces exist in this world that affect us, but that we can't normally see: ghosts, spirits, fairies, presences, otherworldly forces. If scientists believe in quarks and neutrinos because their experiments confirm their existence, then I believe in spirits and supernatural forces because of all the stories I have read and been told from too many sources for it all to be fabrication. When you hear an eighty-year-old Native elder talk about waiting for all the spirits to enter the sweat lodge before closing the door, you get a shiver of appreciation for a dimension of the world that most of us ignore. It's more sensible to dismiss supernatural experiences as irrational wish-fulfilment, just like we dismiss déjà-vu, prophetic dreams, and intuition.

That's why, when I had my film developed and my photograph of St. Brigid's Well was marred by a white blotch, I didn't give it a second thought, except to be disappointed. But when I showed the photographs to friends, someone asked me, "What's this in the picture?"

I said, "Probably my thumb."

"No, it can't be your thumb because there's a piece of vine hanging down over it."

I had another look at it. The white part was grainy, like a milky cloud, and the pattern of the stone seemed still to be visible behind it. It partially blocked the area I most wanted to photograph: where all the flowers and statues had been placed. A dark tendril of ivy curled down and over the white shape.

The photo was handed around.

"It looks like the shadow of a person standing there."

That's exactly what it does look like—the pale shadow of a head, shoulders, arm, and hip of someone standing beside and slightly in front of me, looking into the well.

I've looked at the picture many times since and had many opinions on it. It can't be the reflection of a flash-bulb, a cloud of overexposure, or my thumb, all because of the little curl of ivy at the top, nudging it into the realm of sasquatch and Loch Ness sightings. The fact is, no one can explain it rationally. But the more I look at it, the less I want an explanation, rational or otherwise. When I look at the photograph, it gives me a chill of longing. Maybe once I really was standing there beside something miraculous.

6

ALONE IN GALWAY CITY

[Those] who plead ignorance perpetuate their own belief in the great lie of their ancestors.

—GEORGE MANUEL, *THE FOURTH WORLD*

EVERYONE TOLD ME I HAD TO GO to Galway City. My guidebook called it "delightful." The musicians in the Aille River Hostel raved about the pubs and "the crack," which seems to be something like good conversation, or generally just good times in good company. Anyone I met said, "Have you been to Galway, then?"

I hadn't been to Galway. Actually, I'd planned to skip Galway City and go right on to Clifden, a tempting little village on my map, on a bay even farther out in the

Atlantic than Doolin, and nestled below Connemara
National Park and the famous Twelve Bens. Uppercase
names on maps make me nervous. When I was in France,
I went to Paris out of a sense of duty, and only when I was
down to my last twenty Canadian dollars and on my way
to the airport in Amsterdam. I know that's a pathetic way
to see Paris. But when I travel alone, and especially on a
tight budget, which is the only way I've ever travelled
outside of North America, cities make me unbearably
lonely. During the day, you can wander the shops, go to
museums, soak in the café culture, but at night . . . What
do you do at night?

If I was a man, I would wander into seedy parts of town
peopled only by locals, drink my beer with my back to the
wall, and strike up conversations with strangers without
worrying that they might follow me back to my hotel. I
would be like Humphrey Bogart in *Casablanca:* inde-
pendent, enigmatic, no loyalties. But I am not a man. I am
a small, fine-boned woman with red hair and a freckled
face. I dress practically, in chinos, baggy shirts, and sensible shoes. Experience tells me that I must look timid,
lonely, approachable. I have a bad habit of meeting
people's eyes. Sometimes smiling.

Once when I asked a man for directions in Arles, he
nodded genially, led me into a blind alley, and grabbed me
in a buttocks hold. Luckily, when I slugged him in the chest
with my guidebook, he looked genuinely surprised and
didn't chase me when I ran. A local boy followed me home
and hung outside my hotel room door for hours once in

Guadalajara. I had no phone, and my room opened onto a dark roof away from other rooms. I sat in the dark and waited for him to go away. On a little row boat on the southern coast of Portugal, a toothless old ferryman of about eighty, with skin worn off in patches from the sea salt, tried to row me away to a deserted part of the beach, pleading that his wife was dead and he was lonely. I tried to decline politely but ended up shouting madly to the people who were taking their coffees on the seawall.

In a bed and breakfast in Northern Ireland, the hostess asked me where I'd travelled in Ireland. I told her, then she said, "You're a plucky gurl all right." I'd like to think of myself as a plucky gurl, but there's a fine line between plucky and stupid, and I've crossed it a few times. It seems to me you have to, as a female traveller, unless you can afford to stay in expensive hotels and drink gin and tonics in the lounge every evening and see the world through the window of a tour bus.

I was chastised for my plan to skip over Galway City. The Irish were inordinately proud of this cosmopolitan gem, much more so than of Dublin. The city teemed with history, music, theatre, and bookshops; the streets were narrow, and many people spoke Irish. Fellow travellers praised the good hostels. I had the feeling that my trip was being commandeered by Ireland. So many must-sees clamoured to be squeezed in, and my own agenda was growing fuzzy.

I caught "Brian's bus" to Galway. I had worried about getting a seat in the minibus, but it turned out I was the only passenger. I sat up front and talked to Brian, a friendly, knowledgeable man who waxed poetic about Galway as we drove through the lonely hills along the coast. He insisted that the best music in Galway would be found in the pubs on the other side of the River Corrib, away from the main tourist area.

I'd also been told that I must stay at the Salmon Weir Hostel. I had been spoiled by kindness in the Aille River Hostel in Doolin, and so it was my measuring stick to judge the rest. In my mud-spattered boots and wrinkled khakis, I hauled my pack up the street to the door. It was open, and several young men were lounging proprietarily in the doorway drinking their beer. They were threateningly handsome, like boys from a high-school football team, tall, smooth-skinned, well dressed. It reminded me of a fraternity house, although I've never been near a real one.

"Looking for something?" one asked.

The pack on my back might give it away, I thought, but I answered, "Yes, a bed for one night."

"We're full," he said.

Travelling alone can make you paranoid, but I got the distinct feeling I'd been judged and found wanting. These big clean boys in the doorway were the social committee, checking for the right kind of people at the door.

I found another hostel, modern and warm and bright, with good showers, but nothing at all like Aille River. I was not off to a good start in Galway.

I ate in a vegetarian restaurant like any vegetarian restaurant in any cosmopolitan town, then wandered

Galway, feeling aimless, restless, misdirected. The young men here had close-shaved heads and single earrings, and they wore their pants rolled up at the bottom, in an appealing classic Irish swagger. The women, too, looked classic Irish, with thick kinky hair frizzing softly around their faces in the humidity, eyes that had taken on the hue of the sea and sky, and skin so fresh it was almost translucent, brushed lightly across the nose with freckles. They were dressed in colours as muted as the rain: greys, olives, soft dark purples. The tourists stood out because they clashed with the landscape in their red or turquoise sports fleece, hot pink and green florals, pastel yellows and sunny blues. As for me, I might have looked like a local in my well-worn brown raincoat if it wasn't for my bewildered, "lost tourist" expression. I turned my attention to the shops crammed with Aran sweaters. The Aran ones were out of my league, but I bought a thick wool sweater against the damp June chill. Nothing like shopping to fill in the holes of uppercase name alienation.

Evening was coming on, and I thought I'd go back to the hostel to put on my new sweater and warm up before going out to the pubs. Hassan, a small man of about twenty-five with close-cropped black hair and cinnamon-coloured skin, was warming his feet by the stove.

"Are you Moroccan?" I asked him.

"How did you know?" he said in a thick French accent.

"Just guessed. How do you like Ireland?"

He shook his head at the stove while he searched for words. "It . . . is . . . the . . . worst . . . place I have ever been," he said finally.

I was shocked. The only people I'd heard disparage Ireland were the Irish themselves.

"Why do you say that?"

"I am . . ." He held up his thumb and wagged it.

"Hitchhiking?"

"Yes. Today I stand on the road for hours. In the rain. Nobody stop. I walk maybe fifteen miles to here."

"Really?" I said.

"Everyone tells me the Irish people are so friendly, it's easy to get rides here," he said in disgust.

I wasn't sure what to say because I knew. And I could see that he knew. But he wasn't saying, and neither was I, that in a land of women with beautiful dewy complexions with light sprinklings of freckles across the nose, beautiful brown-skinned folks are less than appreciated. I had already noticed the overwhelming racial uniformity of the places I'd visited in Ireland, but I assumed that Ireland up to then hadn't been thriving economically and attracting immigrants. I found out later that activists in Ireland criticize the government for having an unstated immigration policy that makes it hard for non-whites to settle there.

Hassan's bewilderment made me squirm. How could the Irish, who so bitterly resented the discrimination they had been subjected to, themselves turn discriminators? It was the question I asked myself about my own family history, the question I found I couldn't escape, even here in Ireland. How did my ancestors leave behind the punishing restrictions on their culture, only to find themselves in

North America, if innocently, in a similar role to the British colonizers they so detested at home?

In Ireland in 1695, a series of laws, known as the Penal Laws, was passed by the Protestant Parliament. The laws didn't pretend to try to convert Catholics; instead, they made Catholics into slaves and peasants in their own country. No Catholic could sit in Parliament or vote for members of Parliament. They could not become lawyers or judges. They were not allowed to keep their own schools, could not attend Trinity College in Dublin, and could not send their children away for education. Catholics could not own or carry guns, acquire land from Protestants, or marry Protestants. In fact, in 1752 the law refused to recognize any marriage unless it was performed by the Church of Ireland.

I couldn't imagine how a law like that would affect Catholics like my mother or grandmother. Even in 1982, when I married for the first time, I knew it would not feel like a real marriage to my mother unless it was blessed by the Catholic Church. Some Irish, in the years when the Penal Laws were breaking down, would be married twice: first by a priest, then by a minister. That practice goes on in Canada today among some First Nations couples, who are married in a traditional ceremony, then hold a civil one to make it legal. My second marriage, for instance, performed by a Shuswap elder, is not recognized by Canadian law.

In Ireland in the eighteenth century, Catholic landowners were forbidden to bequeath whole estates; instead,

they had to divide them up, a clever way of making sure
that Catholics lost their status, power, and ability to
support themselves. But probably most damaging of all
was the punishment of the spirit. They were forbidden to
make religious pilgrimages or visits to holy wells, those
distinctly Irish expressions of Catholicism. Contraveners
could be punished by flogging. For practising their faith,
Catholics were turned into criminals in their own land.

Edmund Burke, political philosopher and secretary for
Ireland in the mid-eighteenth century, referred to the Penal
Laws with irony when he called them "a system of wise
and elaborate contrivance, as well-fitted for the oppression, impoverishment and degradation of a people, and
the debasement in them of human nature itself, as ever
proceeded from the perverted ingenuity of man." But if he
thought those bald-faced discriminations were so clever,
he really would have marvelled at the benign-faced inven-
tiveness of Canada's Indian Act.

Before the Indian Act was introduced, the British
government had recognized aboriginal people as self-
governing and dealt with them as nations requiring British
"protection." But in 1876, the Canadian government
implemented the Indian Act, which not only stipulated
that non-Indians would decide who was an Indian and
who wasn't, according to the British system of kinship,
but also aimed to take control of all aspects of Indians'
lives and affairs. The original goal of the Indian Act was
to "encourage the gradual civilization" of Indians, an aim
that was later revised to their "gradual enfranchisement"

or assimilation. Indians could demonstrate that they had attained the European ideal of individualism by embracing the concept of private property. By passing a series of tests, including one proving that he could read and write in French or English (something many white settlers could not do), an Indian could earn a "location ticket," which gave him a piece of land from his reserve. If in three years he proved that he would use it according to Euro-Canadian standards, he would be enfranchised and given title to the land. That also meant he would lose his status as an Indian. On their own land, Indians could not vote until 1960 without losing their status.

No stories survive in my family about the Penal Laws. But in David's family, his grandmother lived through the changes that the Indian Act brought. She remembered how she was given an English name in residential school, and how her father, Moo-um-kim, fought to keep their family names and pass them on. Moo-um-kim also fought to keep their traditions alive. He held potlatches in spite of the prohibitions against them, was thrown in jail by the Indian Agent, then came out and did the same thing all over again.

The similarities to the Penal Laws in Ireland are unnerving. It's hard to imagine that, having been forced to live under the evil laws of some land- and power-greedy intruders in Ireland, the Irish in their new home would allow the subjugation of a people just as fiercely attached to their own land and spirituality. I know that from a distance it's easy to see history large, to see innumerable complexities shaped into coherent patterns with clear causes and effects. I think history also happens small—individual families fighting poverty, hunger, debt, loss of the homes they've known a lifetime. But when my ancestors came to Canada, did they see irony in their position as claim-stakers in a "new" land? Fleeing oppression themselves, did they, like kids on a playground happy to be made part of the bullies' team, join in the oppression with a guilty sense of relief that it wasn't them?

IN SASKATCHEWAN, I WAS REMINDED that while my ancestors might have been ignorant of their role at the time, I couldn't ignore it now. In Regina, David and I lived in the middle of a story of discrimination that hasn't ended.

Before we moved to Regina, we had been warned that we would find racism, all kinds of racism, to be as much a part of the Saskatchewan landscape as the big sky: Cree towards non-Cree aboriginals, whites towards aboriginals, aboriginals towards whites. A Cayuga friend from Ontario who had lived in Saskatchewan for a while told David that as a West Coast Native, he shouldn't expect to find a welcoming atmosphere of solidarity on the plains. The warnings made us more curious than nervous. Neither of us had any experience living with any real racial tension. In the Fraser Valley and places where David grew up, at least on the surface, it seemed to be peace, love, and understanding among the many First Nations reserves and farmers. As a child in Southern Ontario, if I ever saw an aboriginal person, I didn't know it.

Before moving to Regina, we had only stopped there for about an hour once on a road trip. We went to the Canadian Tire to buy motor oil.

"Sure are a lot of Native people here," David said on our way out of the store.

"I noticed that too," I said.

Then we got in the car and drove on to Winnipeg.

Around 14 per cent of the population in Saskatchewan is aboriginal, largely Cree. Cree is the most widely spoken aboriginal language in Canada. Thanks to their sheer numbers, and Hollywood, the teepees, powwows, and feather headdresses of plains culture came to be seen by many North Americans as representative of what a "real Indian" was. But the stoic Hollywood "noble savage" isn't the only stereotype that maintains a stubborn hold in Saskatchewan.

When we were looking for a house in Regina, our real-estate agent chatted to us about the neighbourhoods we'd want to avoid, never directly saying why. When the conversation turned to David's program at university, the equation of Indian studies plus black hair in a ponytail plus tawny skin suddenly added up in the realtor's mind, and panic twisted his face. We weren't sure what was wrong, why he was stuttering and flushed, till he phoned later. When I answered the phone, he tripped over an apology.

"I didn't know David was Native," he said. "I'm so sorry."

"It's okay," I said stupidly. Suddenly I was clear about what was wrong with the neighbourhoods he told us we should avoid.

On other occasions, my half-hearted Smith laugh has come in handy, like the time my elderly neighbour looked at our parched lawns and suggested David do a rain dance.

"Pardon me?" David said politely.

"A rain dance. You're an Indian, aren't you?"

In these situations, David answers with grace, says something like "We don't do those—at least I don't," and moves on. I, on the other hand, with my outer dialogue of understanding good humour, begin an inner dialogue of self-righteous indignation, assigning blame, covering my own ass. How many times have I been blindsided by subtle insinuations that later have me thinking, I should have said . . . After a while, I bore even myself with it.

But those are the subtle things that make you wonder if you're being paranoid. On the other end of the spectrum is what happened to our friend, a fluent Cree speaker and linguistics student at the Saskatchewan Indian Federated College, where David was also a student. He had become a kind of Saskatchewan ambassador to us, taking us on road trips to his reserve and around the province to watch him run competitively. Once or twice a week, he joined us for a vegetarian supper and we exchanged health advice, topping off the evening by rifling through the cupboards for the perfect herbal tea—immune builder, calcium replenisher, cleanser. One crisp fall night in Regina, he was walking home down a wide street, enjoying the mild buzz from a couple of beers he'd had at the pub and thinking about his training for the long-distance race he would be running that weekend. Suddenly he became aware of four strangers who had crossed to his side of the street. Before he had time to react, they jumped him and began kicking and punching him. A taxi driver saw what was happening and called the police. In the hospital, he was stitched and cleaned. His body was covered with deep bruises, his face puffed beyond recognition. He was so humiliated he didn't leave his apartment for more than a week. When he came to our house, the shock of seeing his gentle face swollen shiny blue, with one eye still closed, sent me to the bathroom to compose myself.

My indignation is a useless sentiment. At the core is a tangled knot of culpability, outrage, and sorrow that I want to make sense of. You want to believe your ancestors were virtuous people: industrious, good-humoured, smart, but kind. No one wants to be the one to say, "Now, we have some interesting characters on the Hitler side of the family." I would like to know what my ancestors knew. Did they understand that their diseases had ravaged the Indian people? Had any of them heard of the order given by Lord Jeffrey Amherst during an uprising in 1763 that left two thousand settlers dead to "infect the Indians with sheets upon which smallpox patients have been lying, or by any other means which may serve to exterminate this accursed race"?

Thomas D'Arcy McGee, an Irish political exile in America in the nineteenth century, wrote, in his book

Catholic History of North America, "After Columbus we came, borne onward by the destiny of humanity, in obedience to the primitive charter of our race—'Go forth and fill the earth and subdue it; and in the sweat of your brow you shall earn your bread.' The Irish emigrant stands on this high ground; and so standing he can look the past fearlessly in the face. He has no cause to be ashamed of his predecessors here. If they founded no exclusive *New Ireland,* the blood of no exterminated Indian tribe rises in judgment against them. . . . They were here, subordinates in power, but principals in labor." I like the high-flying sound of that claim, and I'd like to give a dirty-fingernailed but noble slant to the history I'm trying to piece together. I'd like to blame it on the British, wash my hands of the Indian Act, and slip into the cozy denial that wraps around my certainty that *my* signature isn't on any treaties or any of that ancient history. I could weave a romantic image of the subordinate Irish, dragged along in their famine-tattered innocence to found their little bush farms. But it doesn't last. A hymn of guilt whistles through my certainty.

The Cree professor of Indian studies, Neal McLeod, in his article "Coming Home Through Stories," writes, "Canada is often seen as the destination for people in exile from their homelands. However, the Indigenous peoples within Canada have been forced into exile in two overlapping senses: . . . we have been forced from our lands, and also, through such things as residential schools, [we have] been taken away from our collective memory into an 'internal exile.'" Some dark thing tells me that I will never feel at home on this land until I know how my own stories intertwine with the stories of those who were inhabiting the land when my ancestors arrived.

BACK IN GALWAY, HASSAN was so tired and discouraged from his disillusionment about the fabled friendliness of the Irish that he just wanted to go to bed. I wished him well and let myself out into the cool Galway evening. An aggressive anticipation swelled in the knots of people on the street. Lacking any better plan, I decided to follow Brian the bus driver's advice and cross the bridge to the pubs on the other side. I had about as much enthusiasm for this venture as I do for cold showers. Somehow it seemed unpleasantly necessary. I was obliged to have fun in Galway.

It was dark, and as soon as I had crossed the bridge, it became darker. I realized that I had no idea what kind of neighbourhood I was entering. The streets were wider here than in the cobble-stoned charm of the tourist area, and bare. I saw no one else out walking. The streetlights glowed few and far between. I began to think that in this case, the line between plucky and stupid was very clearly defined, and I'd crossed it when I crossed the bridge. Noisy, well-lit streets over there; deserted, dark ones over here. I felt the dizzying awareness that sometimes washes over the solitary traveller: no one knows where I am.

Up ahead, I saw a warm puddle of dusky yellow light pooling on the sidewalk below a Guinness sign. At the same time, I heard the telltale thrum of voices.

This'll do, I thought, and I ducked into the pub.

The place was dark and crowded with people standing. I could barely make my way to the bar. But unlike Canadian pubs that throb with taped music so loud you can talk only to yourself, Irish pubs throb with the beat of human voices. The Irish are heroically garrulous. Being laconic by nature myself, I am astounded by their rapid-fire banter. No remark passes simply without some witty rejoinder. I stood and sipped the creamy foam from my stout and tried to listen. They shouted over each other's heads and carried on about four conversations all at once. They all seemed to know each other. What, I wondered, could they possibly have so much to talk about that hadn't already been talked about on one of the many other evenings they congregated in this same dark pub?

I did not go unnoticed. "Stranger" registered briefly on the faces that glanced my way. Some of the women tried to smile kindly. I cursed myself for bowing to the pressure to come to Galway. I could be listening to the night birds calling in the green hills around Clifden. Instead, I was feeling absurdly vulnerable in this place where I felt like the only outsider. I wished I had a moustache. I wished I had a cigar. I wished I was invisible.

I downed my stout as fast as I could and left. I don't know what I expected. As if because I looked like these people, it would make me one of them.

7.

ST. PATRICK'S PURGATORY

To the Celtic mind, heaven and earth are interdependent and wondrously interactive. The worlds of spirit and matter enjoy a sacred intimacy. This is the way it had been in pagan times, and even the new religion of Christianity could not change Celtic thinking on the matter.

—TOM COWAN, *FIRE IN THE HEAD*

I HAD PLANNED ST. PATRICK'S PURGATORY (a.k.a. Lough Derg) as a high point of my pilgrimage in Ireland. The lake, in County Donegal, near the Fermanagh border, throbbed highlighter pink every time I opened my map: frightening, beckoning, threatening, tempting. I planned to go and told no one; then changed my mind and laughed with fellow Catholics about how I had planned to go; then changed my mind again and vowed to do it. The Irish people I spoke to all said the same thing: "It's very difficult." A nun I met who'd done it as a girl told me, "Sure, and it might turn you off religion altogether."

The tiny island in Lough Derg has been a place of pilgrimage for Catholics for hundreds of years. Legend claims that St. Patrick was the first pilgrim on the island, some time in the fifth century A.D. The oldest surviving relic found there is the column of what is now St. Patrick's cross, traced with spirals that probably date to the ninth century.

In those days, the pilgrimage started with confession, penance, and a fifteen-day bread-and-water fast, then the pilgrim crawled into a cave for a twenty-four-hour vigil. A rock was rolled in front of the opening to lock the pilgrim in a symbolic prison of purgatory, where he must pray for his soul's release. The cave was three feet wide, ten feet long, and just high enough for a pilgrim to kneel. Church authorities discouraged the cave vigil, mostly because of the wild and dangerous visions that pilgrims described when, and if, they survived.

Today's pilgrimage is a much tamer version of the original. The elements that remain—the asceticism; the wind whipping off the lake, carrying rain and cold and hardship; the fasting; the hypnotic, repetitive prayer recited while circling jagged island rock in bare feet; and the long night vigil—are all St. Patrick's special brand of Catholicism, which was often frowned upon by Rome. But these elements are also what sets Irish Catholicism apart from Catholicism as it is practised in other parts of the world.

About sixteen hundred years ago, raiding Celts from Ireland captured a sixteen-year-old boy named Magonus Sucatus Patricius and took him from his upper-class Christian home in Roman Britain, along with thousands of others, to turn him into an Irish slave to the druid Miliuc maccu Boin. For the next six years, Patrick tended sheep on the isolated mountains of Slemish, County Antrim. He was alone, sometimes barely dressed, cold, and often starving. Though he had ignored his parents' religion at home, and run wild with the freedom of relative wealth, Patrick began to feel that on the mountainside, God "guarded [him], and comforted [him] as a father would his son." Plucked from the only life he had known and left to fend for himself in this desperately foreign land peopled by "barbarians" with strange customs, Patrick clung for comfort to the only shred of his former life he could reach. He writes in his *Confession:* "Every day I had to tend sheep, and many times a day I prayed. . . . And my spirit was moved so that in a single day I would say as many as a hundred prayers, and almost as many in the night, and this even when I was staying in the woods and on the mountain; and I used to get up for prayer before daylight, through snow, through frost, through rain, and I felt no harm, and there was no sloth in me—as I now see, because the spirit within me was then fervent."

The deprivation Patrick experienced day after day on the mountain might have been responsible for the visions he began to have. Spiritual people everywhere deliberately subject themselves to fasts, extremes of heat and cold, and repetitive chants to alter their consciousness and bring themselves into the realm of the Otherworld. In Canada, aboriginal people seeking spiritual awareness may undertake traditional vision quests that are similar to what Patrick experienced against his will. Vision quests involve seeking solitude, especially in remote natural places, like mountainsides or woods. A fast is accompanied by repetitive praying and singing and sleep deprivation.

I wonder if Patrick's interpretation of his visions changed any between the time he spent in the wilds of Ireland and his adult writing of the *Confession*. In between, he would have at least heard about his near contemporary Augustine, bishop of Hippo Regius, who had also written a confession, a much lengthier and juicier one. Philosophers, theologians, and regular men and women widely blame or credit St. Augustine, depending on your perspective, for the influence his idea of original sin has had on Christianity. Matthew Fox, whose book *Original Blessing* tries to repair the Augustinian damage, explains that original sin is not contained anywhere in the Old Testament, especially not in Genesis, where it would seem to have originated.

This was a revelation to me when I first read it. The weird notion that we are born guilty bothered me even as a kid. In catechism classes, I learned that newborn babies could go to hell if they died unbaptized. Baptism, even today, is performed to cleanse the baby of the power of darkness and evil, the sin that Adam and Eve apparently transmitted to us like some deadly virus that springs into action at our birth. It haunted me that tiny newborns could be thrust into eternal flames because of the negligence of their ignorant parents, who never got around to having them baptized. They couldn't even be buried in the same cemetery as "real" Catholics. So finding out that the concept was the invention of a guilt-ridden clergyman was a relief to me.

For one thing, somewhere along the way, my idea of hell had changed. On our farm in Southern Ontario, we had a septic tank out along the side of the house that was occasionally opened up for maintenance. As a small child, I remember seeing that pit of stinking excrement and knowing that that was the hell I heard about at Mass. People who had sinned would be tossed in there and the top put back on. But through the years, hell became a metaphor to me, not a real place of eternal flames and pitchforks and stench. The Church says that the main punishment of hell is being separated from God for eternity. Maybe that is also the Church's way of saying, "It could be a metaphor, if that helps you any." I even had a problem with the metaphor, since the whole idea of divine punishment didn't sit well with me. It seemed too human, like an unreasonable parent who grounds you for being late for supper.

I like St. Augustine. It's hard not to like a guy who as an adult still agonized over the pear he stole from an orchard when he was sixteen: "But it was not the pears that my unhappy soul desired. I had plenty of my own, better than those, and I only picked them so that I might steal. For no sooner had I picked them than I threw them away, and tasted nothing in them but my own sin, which I relished and enjoyed." Reading his *Confessions,* I get the impression that he relishes and enjoys his guilt almost as much. *Confessions* is, as the name suggests, a song of guilt—and not just a song, a paean to guilt, as if admitting to guilt is the best any lousy human being can hope for.

Augustine documents his guilt from the time of his birth. But he couldn't have known the pernicious influence that his confession would have on the Christian world. "Who can recall to me the sins I committed as a baby?" he writes. "For in your sight no man is free from sin, not even a child who has lived only one day on earth." He uses all his rhetorical skills to build the case against the baby who will "cry for everything, including things which would harm him" and throw tantrums against those who try to protect him. He concludes that "this shows that, if babies are innocent, it is not for lack of will to do harm, but for lack of strength." And he asks God, if he was born with sin and guilt, when was he ever innocent? The subtext seems to be a subtle and very human excuse for the stories that are to come, a plea that "I couldn't help myself."

Patrick's *Confession* is in the same spirit, a guilty voice full of contempt for the things that make him human. I wonder if we would have heard a different tale of his spiritual adventures in the wilds of Ireland if it wasn't for Augustine.

One night, Patrick heard a voice in his sleep that told him, "It is well that you fast, soon you will go to your own country. . . . See your ship is ready." In his vision, he saw the ship on the distant coast, about two hundred miles away. After six years with his captor, he just walked away. Patrick claims he "feared nothing until [he] came to that ship."

In Patrick's account of his life, it seems that the pagan sailors who agreed to transport him away from Ireland were the first to notice his state of grace. After their three-day voyage to the Continent, they travelled through ravaged and "deserted country" for twenty-eight days. The hungry captain snapped sarcastically at Patrick, "Tell me, Christian: you say that your God is great and all-powerful; why, then, do you not pray for us? As you can see, we are suffering from hunger; it is unlikely indeed that we shall ever see a human being again." Patrick answered them "full of confidence . . . that this day He may send you food on your way until you be satisfied." Sure enough, a herd of pigs suddenly appeared on the road, and for two nights, the crew ate, fed their dogs, and "recovered their strength." The crew recognized some mysterious power in Patrick, and they offered him wild honey, which, according to the translator Ludwig Bieler, was probably "an act of adoration." Patrick refused it.

Patrick eventually made his way back to his home and his family. But he continued to have prophetic dreams and visions. In one, he received a letter in which "the voice of the Irish" cried out to him: "We ask thee, boy, come and walk among us once more." Patrick seems to have longed for the land of his captivity and spiritual awakening; he determined that his destiny lay in converting the Irish to Christianity. For his formal religious training, he went to Gaul and tried to make up for his lost years of education. He never did become educated to his satisfaction, and in his *Confession,* he calls himself "unlearned" and repeatedly mentions his "ignorance" with humility. Nonetheless, he ended up with the job that no one else really wanted: bishop of Ireland. His superiors thought he was crazy to attempt a Christian mission in such a wild and dangerous place, a place that had been bypassed by the expanding Roman Empire because of the intimidating Irish reputation. Also, church authorities disapproved of his unusual methods and weren't sure he was equal to the job.

Patrick's *Confession* makes it obvious that his mission in Ireland was motivated by sincere affection for the Irish people, and not contempt for their "heathen" way of life. He worried over the women who lived in slavery and admired their courage, for "though they are forbidden to do so, they follow Him bravely." Patrick didn't use coercion, though that was the recommended technique for conversion at the time. He blended the Celtic with the Christian, and many Irish, but not all, converted willingly.

The affection that he bestowed on the Irish was returned by them to their saint. Sixteen hundred years later, his version of Catholicism is still practised in Ireland. The pilgrimage I was undertaking was influenced by St. Patrick's focus on asceticism as a path to grace. On a world map of Ireland in 1492, St. Patrick's Purgatory was the only Irish landmark named. I'd done my reading and thought I knew what to expect: a day of fasting, broken only by one "meal" of black tea and dry toast; a twenty-four-hour vigil with more fasting; and lots of prayer. I can't say exactly what drew me to it. I was a Catholic gone awry; bred-in-the-blood believer of some of the teachings, the rest swept away and shaped by juniper, lodgepole pine, coyote eyes in long grass. Salal, chokecherry, salmonberry. Frog song so loud you can't sleep. Saskatoon berries, northern lights, sun dogs on snapping cold days. Deer as soft as the Cariboo hills. Wild onion, devil's club, kinnikinik. These things were in my blood too, had more power over me than Our Man in the pointy hat in Rome. Maybe that's what drew me to Lough Derg. It sounded like Catholicism I could relate to—a wind-lashed island on a mystical black-water lake where time-worn rocks were as much the icons as bejewelled and polished gold likenesses of a man who, after all, could have passed all *his* riches through the eye of a needle. Without being quite conscious of it, I think I pictured it as a kind of Catholic vision quest.

I FOUND A HOSTEL outside Ballyshannon, on the road to Donegal. I suspected that Donegal was the misremembered "Donovan" County where the Smiths had originated. So though I had no idea how to begin looking for a related Smith here, I was glad that this Lough Derg pilgrimage would take place in this county. In a fast-food place, I ate some chips with curry sauce and made notes of how many pounds I'd spent that day. By staying in a hostel with mattresses that felt as if they were filled with straw and sheets so thin I could see through them, and maintaining a diet of low-cost carbohydrates, I discovered I could stay within my budget. I thought of the austerity as preparation for what was to come.

After my chips, I sat in the hostel kitchen drinking tea and pretending to read. I watched other travellers straggle in and felt myself growing increasingly nervous.

"What's the best way for me to get to Pettigo from here?" I asked Evelyn, the hostel owner, naming the nearby town, instead of Lough Derg, to avoid questions.

"You're not doing Lough Derg, then, are you?" she said, instantly attentive.

"I thought I might try it," I said.

"Sure and you're not," she said, teasing.

"I thought I might." I laughed.

"I did it myself as a girl. It's very difficult, that."

"What's that?" said Liam, who had come in earlier. He was a talkative schoolteacher from Dublin.

"She's doing Lough Derg," Evelyn said.

"Lough Derg, is it? Always wanted to see it."

"How do I get there?" I asked again.

"Oh," said Evelyn. "Just make yourself a wee sign and stand out front here on the road."

"Really?" I said. Her suggestion surprised me, since Irish people had cautioned me several times against hitchhiking, whereas the tourists were breezily comfortable with it. I had caught a short ride into Doolin in a busy part of Clare one afternoon from two Irish brothers who lectured me the whole ride on the dangers.

"That's what I would do," Evelyn said.

I thanked her but felt uneasy with the idea. The road out front was a busy highway, with trucks rolling by. I didn't know what the road ahead was like or how many drivers would be travelling to Pettigo.

When Evelyn left the kitchen, the schoolteacher said confidentially, "I wouldn't be taking that advice. It isn't safe at all. I'll give you a lift myself."

"No, no," I said. "That's very nice of you, but it's too far."

"Always wanted to see it myself," Liam insisted. "I've got the weekend off. Lots of time."

"Maybe I can catch a bus," I suggested.

"Oh no, you'd have to go in to Donegal first for that. No, I'll take you. I'll enjoy the ride. Always wanted to see it myself."

And so I reluctantly accepted his incredible hospitality.

After breakfast the next morning, we set out. Breakfast for me was only tea, since we were supposed to begin our fast at midnight the night before our arrival at Lough Derg. The drive was about twenty miles, but it took an hour. Liam drove slowly, over rolling Donegal hills spread with a riot of purple-pink rhododendrons gone wild, and he kept up a constant nervous chatter, asking me questions about Canada and telling me about his life in Dublin. When the conversation lagged, he began thoughtfully, "Lough Derg, is it? Right, rrright. Always wanted to see it. Meant to do it myself one day. Lough Derg. Mm-hmm. Mm-hmm. Rrright."

But up to the last minute, when we pulled up to the edge of the lake where the ferry was docked, I was changing my mind. I could catch a bus out if I didn't like the looks of it, I told myself. But I got out of the car with my pack, and there was no turning back. No buses were to be seen, and I was acutely conscious of the two-hour detour Liam had made in his weekend plans. And he meant to see me off. So I paid the ten-pound fee and fell into line with the other pilgrims. Liam gave me a bright and hardy wave and drove off.

Some women on the ferryboat said, "Oh, from Canada, are you? And aren't you good, taking time out of your holiday to come here!" I could manage only a nervous laugh. I knew my motives were confused and suspect, probably dominated by curiosity.

Low, dusky purple mountains encircled the lake, empty of any kind of habitation except the cluster of buildings and green-domed basilica on Station Island, where we were headed. During the pilgrim season, June to August, no tourists or sightseers are allowed near the island. The booklet issued to pilgrims mentioned the "pervasive calm" of the lake, but the strangely washed greens, greys, and purples of the landscape felt more desolate than calm to me. Even with daily access to a ferry and bus service on the mainland, I felt the claustrophobia of being stranded,

abandoned to the isolation that would close in behind us
as the ferry sailed away without us.

As we disembarked, each pilgrim was marshalled to the
appropriate dormitory and assigned a bunk in a tiny
closet-like cubicle referred to as a "cell." A grey army-
style blanket was folded neatly at the end of each bed, on
top of paper-crisp white sheets. I was relieved to see that I
didn't have a roommate; the room measured about five
feet by eight feet. We were supposed to take off our
footwear and get settled in for the three days ahead. My
bare feet touched the ice-cold cement floor and I winced.
I tried the tap in the corner sink: cold water only. The
asceticism shook an involuntary shiver of anticipation
from me. I liked the idea of a physical test, my body
involved in the spiritual experience. But later I would be
overjoyed to discover that the women's bathroom on our
floor was not only heated, but also equipped with a
strange row of urinal-looking things that turned out to be
foot-washers with hot water.

The first order of business was to complete several
Stations of the Cross before six o'clock Mass by circling
the penitential rock "beds" that had existed since St.
Patrick's time. I had completely forgotten the details of the
ritual, since I hadn't done Stations of the Cross since I was
about thirteen years old. I'd have to wing it, but I could
see I would need a rosary to keep track of my prayers. I
had left my hand-me-down hanging on the branch at St.
Brigid's Holy Well, back in County Clare. I bought
another in the gift shop, plain black plastic with a silver

Jesus on the crucifix, made in Italy.

I was grateful for the centuries of pilgrim feet that had
smoothed the jagged rocks a little as I started my first
station of standing, walking, kneeling, praying. The
Lough Derg Guide explains that "by the physical activi-
ties of moving round the beds barefooted, of fasting and
staying awake, the whole body takes part in prayer." The
series of prayers consisted of sets of Hail Marys, Our
Fathers, and Creeds. I tried a few, but pretty soon I
adapted my own, because I never did know the whole
Creed by heart, and the repeated prayers lost their
meaning for me in the singsong rhythms that became (and
always had, when I was a kid) "Thy kingdumcum, thy
wilby-dun." But maybe that was the point, the meditation
of it, and I was too concerned with trying to get it right to
surrender to it. The Irish pilgrims' voices rose and fell,
smoothly up and over the words, looping around and
starting again.

I looked out at the tossing black lake and listened to
the wind rushing through the four-hundred-year-old
sycamore trees. I tried to find some peace in the connection between nature and spirituality that was supposed
to be a part of Celtic Christianity. I marvelled at the age
of the rock underfoot, and I tried to muster up some
spark of sincere feeling for what seemed at that moment
like a profoundly ridiculous ritual. The iron crucifixes
inspired a hint of awe, and I knelt before them, trying
not to mind the pointy stones jabbing into my knees. But
the thought of kissing them, as other pilgrims did, made

me barely contain a shudder. Too flashy, too public, too over the top—not to mention the germs.

The day so far had stayed sunny, but fierce winds from the lake battered us with cold. Later it would blow in dark clouds and rain. The pilgrims seemed undaunted. I can't generalize about the pilgrims I saw at St. Patrick's Purgatory, except to say that I think I was the only non-Irish there. The bare feet that circled the ancient stones were some of them old and yellow and craggy and bleeding, some of them young and pink and mottled with cold, some with bandaged toes, some callused, some with manicured and painted nails.

After the Stations of the Cross, there was time for a tea break before Mass. Teenagers with their parents gathered around the cafeteria tables; single men and middle-aged women, pairs of older women, husbands and wives—all chatted about other pilgrimages, named friends and relatives they had in common. We all drank several cups of black tea and ate our fill of oatcakes, which, though bland and dry as dust, tasted delicious after a day without food. An air of holiday celebration buzzed gently through the hall. The pilgrims could barely contain their eagerness to get started on the faith endurance test. From the people I spoke to over our last meal, I knew that the reasons for coming to Lough Derg were as varied as the feet. Some had begun to feel doubts and needed to reaffirm their faith. Others had been coming back, religiously, every year, and looked forward to that three days of spiritual peace in the midst of their busy lives. I couldn't help feeling that all of them had remarkable faith to even be there, and that this was a distinctly Irish kind of pilgrimage. I was uneasy. I was supposed to be uneasy, that was the point, but it wasn't just the asceticism of the place. I wanted to hide the little Canadian flag pin that adorned the daypack I carried. It announced me for what I was: definitely a foreigner here, maybe even a trespasser.

After the evening Mass and prayers, we prepared for the long vigil through the night. The wind blew in bursts, peppering rain on the cold stone walkways where we hurried with purple-cold feet to get warm clothing to layer on as the cold deepened. We had been warned that we would not be able to return to the dormitories during the night. Once we committed to the vigil, we were in for the long haul, inexorably drawn into a spell of repentance, trapped in a symbolic prison of purgatory, waiting for the dawn. The vigil would take place in the unheated basilica, whose stone floor was icier than the walks outside. But at least we'd be protected from the rain.

Once all the pilgrims were inside the basilica, the tall doors were pulled to with a hollow finality. This is symbolic of the early days of the cave, when penitents were literally locked in for twenty-four hours. (Wild old rumours whisper that some pilgrims were never found when the cave was opened after the vigil.) Pilgrims are no longer locked in; you are free to decide for yourself if you want to slip outside for fresh air.

The prayers inside were the same, but this time they were recited aloud, as we walked in circles around the inside of the church. It was hard to keep my mind on the prayers; I found myself wondering about the everyday lives of these men and women following one after another in a line, rosaries swinging from their hands, their pant legs neatly rolled up to keep from stepping on hems. I tried to imagine a parallel to this in Canada. Some people raced through the words of the prayers, skipping whole phrases as they went. The hum was hypnotic, a hive of bees buzzing with Hail Marys. I remembered my grandparents sitting by the raspberry bushes every evening on their farm in Ontario, saying the rosary this same way, lilting and falling. Grandma used to start, calmly, quietly, with the "Hail Mary full of grace" while my grandpa sat apparently snoozing till his cue, "the fruit of thy womb, Jesus," when he'd suddenly snap to attention with a booming "*Holy Mary,* mother of God!" like a curse.

After we had done maybe two hours of walking and praying, my feet looked mottled, like ham slices lost too long in the back of the fridge. I could smell pungent frankincense hanging in the air, and the sharp old odour of church pews. When I was a kid and my hands sweated holding onto the back of the pew in front of me while I thought up sins for confession, that acrid wood odour burnt my nostrils. It burned them now. I couldn't keep up with the prayers. I slipped my rosary into my pocket and pulled my wool cap lower over my ears.

The Gaelic poet Fearghal Og Mac an Bhaird called St. Patrick's Purgatory "a cave that cures men of stiff pride." My stiff pride had already sustained a deflating jab. I was trying hard to surrender to the intimacy and magic of this odd collective act—the humble, mumbling crowd of pilgrims circling the church interior monotonously, stepping repeatedly over wooden kneeling benches, bumping knees and shins against the pews as we rounded the corner once again. But instead I found myself working up a defensive attack on something I couldn't really understand.

I slipped out of line and let myself out into the cold night. Other pilgrims were outside too, helping each other out with words of encouragement, but I kept to myself. My resolve to learn something from this pilgrimage, to rekindle a flicker of Catholic faith, had dissolved into grim perseverance. By about three in the morning, I was chilled to the bone, hungry, tired, displaced. I tried to shift my status to curious observer, a tourist who'd breached security, but even that couldn't sustain me. I made frequent trips to the bathroom, just to have an opportunity to be alone and sit down without that monotonous humming noise following me. On one of those trips, I discovered I had part of a chocolate bar crumpled at the bottom of my knapsack. All pretense completely gone, I sat on the toilet and ate it.

Earlier, I had stood outside with my arms outstretched against the church wall and renounced the world, the flesh, and the Devil. This is supposed to mean a renewal of promises made at baptism, but I had no more understood the act than if I had slipped into a secret Masonic temple meeting. I had the feeling that, though in theory I would renounce the Devil if I thought it would help, I was all for the world and the flesh. I grew up with the Catholic sin test that Matthew Fox mentions in *Original Blessing*: "Did you take pleasure in it?" If you did, it was supposed to be a sure sign of sin. I share Fox's conviction that, on the contrary, delight must be a positive thing, a blessing and not a sign of sin. But delight did not have a place in the religion I learned.

When I was thirteen and starting junior high school, my parents decided to send me to a private Catholic school. I was very shy, and after seeing my sisters' experiences at the neighbourhood junior high, my mother worried that I would have a hard time there. So she hemmed my navy blue uniform, and I sewed on the crest and took the city bus out to the edge of Winnipeg, to St. Charles Academy. It wasn't an exclusive private school; my parents paid about thirty dollars a month to send me there. There must have been a family rate, because whole large Catholic families attended. I loved it. Every Friday, we attended Mass at the school chapel. I got to be an altar girl with my friend Andrea. Andrea was one of those girls who could get you laughing hysterically without ever cracking a smile herself. Pure fear kept me from laughing when we performed our duties at the altar. But back in the regular pews, Andrea entertained herself by trying to get me to laugh. She knew not to whisper in my ear, because that would get her in trouble. Instead, she made quacking motions with her hands when the priest spoke and quacked back with the other hand when we responded. My body shook, but I held it in. So she rolled her socks right down to the tops of her shoes and sat there with her legs crossed as if nothing was odd. I let loose with one of those laughs that explodes through the nose. One of the nuns came and grabbed my ear and pulled me out of the church. I had never been, and was never again, grabbed by the ear. It was humiliating. And the sock thing wasn't even funny. But that's the thing about humour in a Catholic church: there isn't any. I was betrayed by my uncontrollable desire to laugh. As St. Patrick says, "The hostile flesh is ever dragging us unto death, that is, towards the forbidden satisfaction of one's desires."

The thought of confession, which was to follow at daybreak on Lough Derg, hard on the heels of the vigil, also troubled me. It's not that I don't believe in these things, awry though I may be. I respect rituals that pay attention to the details of life, our relationship with others, and with a creator; that acknowledge our humility and our gratefulness. But I hadn't been to confession in so long that I didn't know what I considered a sin any more. As I circled the basilica, I thought about it. There were the seven deadlies: pride, lust, greed, anger, gluttony, covetousness, and sloth. Sure, I'd transgressed in a few of those areas, especially if sloth meant lying in bed till noon on a Saturday listening to "Basic Black" on the radio. But the level of my transgression didn't really seem like sin to me. Sorcery and idolatry were two sins that seemed to me very open to interpretation. And I remembered the phrase "in word, thought, deed, or omission." Omission. That one really hit home.

But that and the other things I was really ashamed of were not things I would be comfortable telling a stranger's profile shadowed behind a screen. I had adapted another way to make my peace for the things I think of as sins. Like the Celts, I find comfort in bringing offerings to a sacred spring and unloading my sorrow at a fairy lake. Under a cedar tree or with the wind hissing through prairie grass, it feels like something divine is listening.

St. Patrick's cold and deprivation reminded me of my uncle Neil's gentle caution about Irish-Catholic fervour, the caution I had ignored at the time. I had come here looking for some way to salvage my Catholicism, but I had to admit I was a tourist, my heart and my understanding not in it. Maybe the full meaning of the term "penitential" had slipped by me when I'd prepared for my pilgrimage, like storm warnings you ignore in your haste to get away for a summer long weekend. The wildness of nature here was not a path to bring us closer to God, but was relished as St. Patrick relished it, as a particularly gruelling route to self-punishment: tactile, visual, a sensual "Act of Contrition." Nature was the instrument of our torture, our hair shirt and briar whip. If my feet rigor mortised into purple cubes of flesh, I should bite my lip and know I deserved it.

Passing the doors on another round, I took my opportunity and slipped out of the basilica for good. I made my way cautiously in the dark along the stone walls to the women's dormitory. The lake roiled in black beyond the penitential beds; the sycamores moaned in the wind. An image of purgatory learned in childhood seized me suddenly, a terrifying grey gulf filled with tortured, clambering souls trapped a hair's breadth from heaven. At the dormitory door I hesitated, said a prayer that it wouldn't be locked. It wasn't.

My raw bare feet climbed the stairs silently. I stopped in the bathroom, where a stir of sudden heat sent a warming tingle through my chilled bones. In my "cell" in the dark, I burrowed under papery sheets and listened to the wind toss rain against the window in this place that was a thousand years Irish. Then from my pack, I dug out a sweat-polished stone. I remembered the warm smell of sun on skin the day I had fished the stone from the Chilliwack River. I remembered holding my body steady in the current of shocking cold, mountain meltwater. As I held the stone in my hand, I felt it warm up and my heartbeat calm.

The next day in the drizzling morning rain, I hoisted my pack to my back and boarded the first ferryboat to touch the shore.

NORTHERN IRELAND

*Nothing is more difficult in Irish history than to try and distinguish
reality from myth.*

—ROBERT KEE, *IRELAND: A HISTORY*

WHEN I REACHED THE SHORE, A BUS was waiting to
take pilgrims into Pettigo. From there I went on to
Donegal town, where the bus pulled up in front of a nice
hotel. Tired of self-denial, tired of my budget, I walked in
and booked myself a room. It cost eight times what my
last hostel had cost. But when I walked in the room and
saw that solid queen-sized bed with the big comforter,
good clean sheets, and fluffy pillows, not to mention the
private bathroom and TV, I didn't care. It had started to

rain. I ran myself a hot bath, soaked for a good long time, then slathered myself with hotel moisturizer. I ordered tea and a sandwich, then I got into bed completely warm and dry, and watched TV and the rain.

The next day, with a backpack full of clothes fresh from the laundromat, I waited outside the hotel for a bus to Derry. A confusion of tourists crowded the sidewalk with their luggage. Tour buses and Eireann buses lined up in all directions, changing their destination signs, pulling away. I had no idea which bus to board, so I asked a driver.

"You wouldn't be going to Derry, would you?"

"You're dead right I wouldn't," he said seriously, then he cracked a wide smile.

A social worker from Dublin had also told me he wouldn't go to Northern Ireland, despite the ceasefire. "I can't get used to having a nineteen-year-old British soldier aiming a gun at me at the border," he said.

I felt a little nervous about getting on a bus to Derry, Northern Ireland, myself. In the sixties and seventies, I had heard the name Londonderry in the news again and again, usually along the lines of "fighting in the streets of Londonderry," and in 1972, when the sinister words "Bloody Sunday" bathed the radio and TV. On that day, Sunday, January 30, thousands of Irish demonstrators marched in the streets of Derry, protesting the British government's use of internment without trial or charge and the ban on public demonstrations. What was supposed to be a non-violent protest took a brutal turn when British soldiers fired into the crowd and killed thirteen apparently unarmed people, eight of whom were under twenty years old. I was only ten and didn't pay much attention to the news, but the name Londonderry had a musical ring that caught my imagination. But until I came to Ireland, I didn't realize that, far from being musical, the name Londonderry holds out a political challenge to Irish Nationalists and Protestant Unionists alike.

In the sixth century, the famous Irish saint Columcille founded a monastery on the city site, where an oak grove grew. Like the pagan Celts, Columcille found something naturally sacred in the oaks, and the place was named Doire, Gaelic for oak. The name later became anglicized to Derry, and it remained an innocent, peaceful, even sacred name until the seventeenth century. During the Ulster Plantation, when Protestant English and Scottish colonizers were handed over Irish land in the northern counties, architects, builders, and tradesmen from London were granted large chunks of land in Derry to build a merchant centre. In their honour, the town was renamed Londonderry, and the peaceful history of the name took a nasty turn. Today, pro-British loyalists brazenly call the city Londonderry, pushing their status as power-holders in the faces of most other people, who prefer Derry, discarding the colonizer's challenge and returning the name to its origins. On National Geographic and RandMcNally maps of Ireland, the city is still called Londonderry. And though the BBC news network has begun to alternate between the two names, the CBC in Canada stubbornly hangs on to Londonderry.

I sided with the underdogs myself and preferred Derry. But the struggle to insist that names matter reminded me of the irony in my ancestors' story. Around Lake Ontario, a host of indigenous names, like Ashquasing (meaning "that which lies at the end"), Nanzuhzaugewazog (meaning "having two outlets"), and Noossiquawaunk (meaning "salt lick where deer resort"), had been replaced with English names like Twelve Mile Creek, Sixteen Mile Creek, and Forty Mile Creek.

The bus headed to Derry approached the border into Northern Ireland. The passengers seemed calm; this was routine for many of them, who crossed the border every day. So maybe it was only me imperceptibly holding my breath as we faced the most intimidating border crossing I'd ever encountered. Imposing barricades narrowed the road to a single lane. Behind us towered a high fence strung with loops of razored barbed wire and mounted with surveillance cameras. Armed military stood on guard. I had a hard time reconciling that kind of military readiness with the Ireland of rolling green hills where I had wandered, alone and unbothered, day after day. And this was during the ceasefire.

As we came into Derry, traffic slowed. The bus passed the shell of a bombed-out building fenced in by barbed wire and topped with an Irish flag flying at half-mast. It was hard to tell if some buildings had been bombed or were just crumbling from neglect, maybe because I couldn't quite believe I'd just crossed the line into a place where bombs were part of the landscape. We passed a two-storey wall mural of a giant Irish-coloured (orange and green) screw going through a British-coloured (red and blue) soldier's helmet. Political murals have been a prominent feature on Derry walls since the seventies, splashing passersby with Loyalist and Nationalist symbols and slogans. Across the towns of Northern Ireland, hundreds of murals carry the same messages: "Still defending Ulster. We will always be ready." "Free Ireland." "1688–1690. Faith Hope and Charity. This we maintain. No popery!" Northern Irish Catholics and Protestants walk every day beneath the murals, drive by them, see new ones springing up as frequently as billboards advertising underwear and cellphones. They are constantly reminded that the religion they practise, much as they might like to ignore it, somehow implicates them in this political battle.

Because in Ireland, you can't separate religion and politics. Even the act of wearing a crucifix around your neck is not just something that gives you private comfort and reassurance; it can also be a political statement, a banner of pride and defiance, a reminder to the oppressor that he hasn't succeeded.

As traffic thickened and our bus crawled more and more slowly along the thoroughfare, eventually stopping with a hiss of airbrakes, I noticed an increasing police presence. I tried to gauge the other passengers for signs of alarm; people were craning their necks and growing impatient. I could have imagined it, but I thought I sensed a flicker of concern travelling through the bus.

Then, between buildings, my eye caught a blur of racing bikes streaming by on the next street over. It turned out that the World Cup Triathlon was on, and streets had been blocked off for the race. The bus station had also been temporarily relocated, and the driver suggested that two German tourists and I head for the train station instead, since it was easier to get to. As the three of us took a short-cut up a stone staircase to the eerily empty street above, the only danger we were in was the danger of being knocked over by a flock of hell-bent cyclists in spandex shorts speeding through the street. But the sense of disorientation over what things seemed to be and what they really were stayed with me throughout my time in Northern Ireland.

While we were waiting for the train, a marching band of about ten young people came parading up the railway tracks, playing their instruments in the June sunshine. That wasn't so odd in itself, but the way the other people waiting at the station pointedly ignored them did seem odd to me. The music wasn't that interesting, but I thought it was pleasant, so like a polite tourist, I tapped my foot as they stopped in front of us. It didn't occur to me until later that June was midway into the marching season, which lasts from April to August in Northern Ireland. This band of young people practising seemed innocent to me but could be a reminder of tension and apprehension to many Derry people. Had I arrived in Derry a month or two later, I would have walked blindly into the thick of a conflict over marching season that even during the ceasefire erupted in violence.

The marching season's images of a charging white horse
and the date 1690 are instantly understood. They both
refer to the defeat of King James II, who, having been
driven from England, returned to Ireland, where he was
welcomed enthusiastically by Catholics. But on July 1,
1690, the new Protestant king, William of Orange,
defeated James at the Battle of the Boyne, near Drogheda.
King William's victory secured Protestant supremacy in
Ireland, and ushered in an era of persecution and suffering for Catholics that included the infamous Penal Code.

After King William's victory, the colour orange became a
symbol for Irish Protestants who wanted to celebrate their
loyalty to the British crown. The colour also became the
name of a secret society, the Orange Order, whose members
made it their mandate to protect Protestant interests from
"a catholic society perceived to be continually subversive,"
as historians Cecil Houston and William Smyth write. They
modelled their fraternity on the Masonic Lodges, right
down to the grand masters, secret oaths and signs, rituals,
and passwords. Besides marching every July 12 to celebrate "King Billy's" success, eighteenth-century Orangemen
took it upon themselves to terrorize Catholics who
refused to renounce their faith. They burned Catholic
chapels, conducted night-time raids on Catholic homes to
search for arms, and nailed threats on Catholics' doors,
ordering them to vacate Protestant territory with the cry
"To hell or Connacht!" I wonder if my great-grandparents
living in the northern counties ever lay in their beds on a
foggy Irish night, listening to peacock howls and moans of

distant wind and surf, waiting for the out-of-place sounds
of human voices, coming closer.

These days, some Orangemen like to put a cleaner spin
on their image. Some insist the Orange fraternity is not
about sectarian divisions, but is about celebrating their
Protestant heritage, eating hamburgers in the sunshine,
and listening to the marching bands play good old tunes
like "The Sash My Father Wore" and "The Protestant
Boys." But in their oath, Orangemen promise "to give no
countenance, by [their] presence or otherwise, to the
unscriptural, superstitious, and idolatrous worship of the
Church of Rome." They also "promise never to marry a
Roman Catholic, never to stand sponsor for a child receiv-
ing baptism from a priest of Rome," and "to resist, by all
lawful means, the ascendancy, extension and encroach-
ments of that Church," etc. Even to me, a non-practising
Catholic from elsewhere, there's something creepy about
news reports of huge crowds parading through Northern
Ireland's streets to celebrate the oppression of a people
distinguished by their religious faith. It seems distinctly
different from, say, a St. Patrick's Day parade, which cele-
brates a saint intrinsic to the culture.

When I was nine years old, in 1970, my family took a
trip to South Carolina. Eight of us drove all the way
from Ontario in a Pontiac Parisienne, my dad smoking
fat cigars, us kids singing road songs that had repetition
as their key feature, and my mother keeping the peace.
The South in 1970 really was like a Neil Young song. I
did see tall white mansions and little shacks and a great

big official road sign that said, "You are now entering Ku Klux Klan territory." The sign was shocking enough. But my second-oldest sister, Mary, who was fourteen and had a compulsive reading habit and a love of anything with a dark dramatic twist to it, said, "You know the KKK are against Catholics too." Catholics? I remember the startled disbelief, then the sinking injustice of it— maybe my first experience of feeling "other"—then the fear. That night in our motel room, as we kids drank Orange Crush and read *Ripley's Believe It or Not* comic books on the beds, and Barbie and Pat pretended to be spring-heeled Jack the Ripper, flinging themselves from bed to bed and scaring my little brother, I worked myself into a sweaty panic thinking about the Ku Klux Klan. We knew about the KKK, with their pointy white witch hats and slits for eyes, and their burning crosses and gangs setting fire to black homes and churches. How would they even know we're Catholics? I wondered. And it wasn't until I'd satisfied myself that our Pontiac sitting outside was sufficiently anonymous and no one could tell from our last name, that I could calm down enough to sleep.

For Catholics in Ireland, I don't imagine there's any startled disbelief as Orangemen and Apprentice Boys congregate for their annual solidarity party in the streets of Northern Irish towns. The animosity is so old, it's become routine. The people I met in Northern Ireland didn't want to talk about "the Troubles" at all, except for a cocky Catholic musician from Belfast with a shaved head, army boots, and a prominent crucifix around his neck. When he heard I was tracing my family through Ireland, he asked me my last name. When I told him, he said, "You're not one of those fucking Brits, are you?" I denied all but the thin line on my father's father's side, where my name came from. Most of the other people I met gave me the sense of a deliberate, studied denial, and a holding of breath for a fragile peace.

I didn't plan to stay in Belfast, because I had run dangerously low on funds and I always spent too much money in cities. But when I arrived, the first thing I saw as I walked out of the train station was the Belfast Grand Opera House that's pictured on the front of a Van Morrison album. It's a beautiful red brick building decorated with elaborately detailed cream trim: round and half-circle windows in leaded and stained glass, onion-shaped spires, curlicue spindles and arches, and a bronzy-hued atrium on one side. It is grand and surreal, perfect for an opera house. I instantly wanted to stay, or least do some walking around. But owing to the Troubles, no lockers existed to store luggage in the Belfast station, which made things logistically difficult. The streets were almost deserted, not many tourists, except for a few back-packers wandering with their unleavable burdens.

I had run out of film, so I hauled my pack into a store, looking for a postcard of the opera house. All I found were a few curled-up postcards that looked as if they were from the 1970s. But I felt like my friend Fred in the still pine forest in the Chilcotin–Cariboo country of British

Columbia: I had a good feeling in this place. Instead of the fear and apprehension I had expected, I felt instantly at ease here. I tried to connect this effect to some cause. Was it the strangely deserted streets? All the Van Morrison songs I knew, wailing through me like some "inarticulate speech of the heart"? I wanted to abandon all my fears of cities and the possibility of being in the wrong place at the wrong time, a tourist caught innocently in an age-old animosity.

I had tended to think that the sectarian strife in Ireland had nothing to do with my family's history. I thought that when they immigrated to Canada, those differences were gladly left behind, and that Catholics took their place alongside Protestants—and good riddance to Penal Laws, prejudice, and marching in the streets to celebrate July 1690. In 1852, Susanna Moodie wrote, "The old quarrel between Irish Catholics and Protestants should have been sunk in the ocean when they left their native country to find a home, unpolluted by the tyrannies of bygone ages, in the wilds of Canada." I thought it had been. They might see haunting echoes of their experience in the Indian Act and the laws against aboriginal religious practices. But I had assumed that for my ancestors, those days of religious intolerance were over.

I had no reason to think otherwise, growing up in 1960s Ontario. I lived insulated in a cocoon of Catholicism. Sunday was a ritual of putting on a good dress, knee socks, good shoes, and a hat or lace chapel veil over my hair. My brother and I pulled a wagon up and

down the driveway, trying not to scuff our shoes, as we
waited for the rest of the family to get ready for Mass. In
the church, the priest's voice hummed through familiar
words that formed a pattern of sounds long before they
made any sense. Each week, we went through the same
loops of sitting, standing, and kneeling. My mother and
father struck their chests to humble themselves. My sister
Barbie flipped rapidly through her illustrated Mass missal,
so that the pictures of the priest going through the
motions of the Mass made cartoon callisthenics, and
when I snickered, my parents shot me the evil eye.

At the Catholic school we went to, we were surrounded
by other Catholics—Irish, Polish, Italian, French—who
didn't eat fish on Friday either, knew how to genuflect,
and knew which books were in "the Index." They too
walked around with a smear of ashes on their foreheads
on Ash Wednesday, propped palm branches behind the
religious pictures in their bedrooms, and had their throats
blessed with a cross of white tapers on February 3. Instead
of a first-aid kit, they had the crucifix on the wall at home,
with a latched compartment in the back containing emer-
gency holy water and oil for Extreme Unction. I had no
sense of Catholics being "outsiders" in any way. My
mother and grandmother kept a careful watch on our new
friends, asking us, "Are they Catholic?" but I wonder now
when I would have even had an opportunity to meet a
non-Catholic. And why they asked. As for non-Catholics,
the main thing I learned was that they were okay to have
as casual acquaintances, but as friends, you would face a

deep chasm of mutual misunderstanding. And forget about marrying one; that would cause no end of trouble.

The only religious persecution came from within. The note I brought home to my mother about our First Communion said we could wear either black or white shoes with our white Communion dresses. Since I had a brand-new pair of black fake suede lace-up shoes, my mother decided I could wear them. I fought with her and begged her to dye them (as I'd seen her do to her own shoes), but she remained firm: the note said we could wear either. That spring morning, all the girls outside on the steps of St. Mary's Church looked like tiny brides in their lacy white veils, puffed sleeves, and frothy skirts. My best friend, Carol, had a flared satiny mini-dress with thigh-high white stockings and a stylish little Jackie Kennedy Onassis veil. My dress and veil, having been worn by two or three sisters before me, wasn't quite 1969 chic, but I loved the swishing sound it made as I walked, and I had decided that the lacy dress would overshadow the shoes. I was wrong. Every girl in my class wore white shoes that day—with knee socks, with leotards, some even with nylons, but all white. To make things worse, Carol and I were the smallest girls in the class, so the photographer placed us smack in the middle of the church steps, right in front. The photograph taken that day shows the almost-perfect symmetry of a row of boys in black and a sea of girls in white, clasping their hands in devotion, then a blob of black that was my shoes, "spoiling the picture," as a friend's mother told her. After the initial blush of humiliation wore off, I bore my persecution the way I'd been taught—it was good for me.

But I didn't know that the cocoon of belonging hadn't always been there. If, in the mid-1800s, my ancestors thought they were leaving the Orange Order and marching season behind in Ireland, they must have been surprised to find that in Upper Canada, the parades and privileges continued with the strongest Orange fraternity in the world, next to Ireland's. In fact, in the nineteenth century, Toronto was sometimes referred to as the Belfast of Canada; Kingston was called the Derry of Canada.

The Orange Order, which came to British North America unofficially sometime around 1800, began mainly as "clubs" to help new Irish-Protestant immigrants get settled, find work, and develop a comforting social network to make them feel at home. In 1830, the order became officially established under the leadership of Ogle Gowan, who tried his best to make it a respectable organization. The Orange Order in Canada has been portrayed as everything from a collection of bigots whose pleasure it was to make life miserable for their Catholic neighbours to loyal good old boys spending their time building insurance funds for their Protestant brothers' unfortunate widows. It seems that the truth lies somewhere in between.

Protestants formed the majority in Upper Canada in the nineteenth century, with Irish Protestants making up the largest group settling in Ontario. So it was natural that an

institution that formed a large part of their cultural identity in Ireland would be transferred to Canada. In 1850,
there were more than forty thousand Orangemen in the
province, and by 1860, it was closer to one hundred thousand. Raging against superstitious papists and "popery,"
and working themselves into anxiety about the threat of a
Fenian invasion, unified Protestants and helped solidify
their identity.

The prejudices of Protestants might have helped shape
the Catholic identity too. Suffering was a point of pride
among Irish Catholics; it was a virtue that led to purifica-
tion. The feeling of being part of a persecuted culture
tapped into a long tradition of Christians being martyred
for their religious convictions. According to writer Greg
Dues, "Tradition indicates that most, if not all, of the
original apostles were put to death" for their beliefs.
Catholics were used to suffering; the Orange Order prejudices were just one more cross to bear that improved their
chances in the hereafter.

Overt, violent discrimination of the kind found in
Ireland was rare in Upper Canada, although it did occur.
Houston and Smyth describe deliberate attempts to keep
Catholics from moving into Protestant townships in
Ontario. A gang called the Town Line Blazers used
various intimidation tactics, including the occasional
burning of property, to keep Catholics away. But as the
authors explain, "Their bullying tactics were replaced in
later decades by more sophisticated economic, political,
and social devices."

In the 1840s, Irish Catholics poured into Upper Canada, fleeing famine in Ireland. Among these Catholics were the majority of my Irish ancestors. From Northern Ireland came Hugh Dillon, from County Antrim in 1840; Owen Leonard, from Fermanagh County; Mary Bethel, from either Armagh or Monaghan; and Hugh Smith, from Monaghan. To them, as historian Hereward Senior explains, "The annual parades of the Orangemen were a reminder of past humiliations and suggested to Catholics an attempt to impose the type of discrimination they had faced in eighteenth-century Ireland." Most Irish Catholics didn't have the option of returning to Ireland. So the paranoia of the Orange Order Protestants, and their attempts to call into question the loyalty of Catholics, would at the least have been a frustration, an obstacle to their blending in with the new landscape.

In 1842, construction was set to begin on a "feeder" to the Welland Canal, with six locks between St. Catharines and Thorold. Hordes of men, mostly Irish famine immigrants, gathered in St. Catharines looking for work, many with their families. When the start of construction was delayed, gangs of hungry men attacked the stores and mills along the canal and in the village of St. Catharines. The Catholic pastor and the Presbyterian minister managed to solicit the charity of the village business owners, mainly Protestants, and the so-called Bread Riots were brought under control. But this and another canal-related riot in 1849, and the perceived threat of that radical Irish group the Fenians, would not have helped the Catholic image any.

Despite some historians' attempts to downplay the bigoted aspect of the Orange Order, for Catholics the discrimination was real. Gregory Kealey writes: "It was clear that in Toronto at least there were a whole series of corporation jobs which were retainers for an Orangeman's faithful service." Orange-controlled jobs included those in the post office, the customs house, the gasworks, the waterworks, and the police and fire departments. At Thanksgiving last year, I listened to my father and my sister-in-law's Catholic parents talking about the jobs in Southern Ontario that, even in their memory, were commonly known to be restricted to Orangemen.

In 1852, Susanna Moodie wrote from Belleville, Ontario, "These hostile encounters [Orange parades] are of yearly occurrence in the colony and are justly held in abhorrence by the pious and thinking portion of the population of either denomination. . . . [They] effectually prevent any friendly feeling which might grow up between members of these rival and hostile creeds." But in spite of Moodie's conviction, her own perception of Catholics is telling: "It is a solemn thing to step into their churches, and witness the intensity of their devotions. Reason never raises a doubt to shake the oneness of their faith. They receive it on the credit of their priests, and their credulity is as boundless as their ignorance. . . . I cannot but respect their child-like trust. . . . [The Catholic] has imposed upon himself a heavier yoke than the Saviour kindly laid upon him, and has enslaved himself with a thousand superstitious observances which to us appear absurd. . . . If the

Protestant would give up a little of his bigotry, and the
Catholic a part of his superstition . . . we should no longer
see the orange banner flaunting our streets on the twelfth
of July, and natives of the same island provoking each
other to acts of violence and bloodshed."

Just as in Northern Ireland, religious differences in
Canada were emphasized every year during parades: St.
Patrick's Day, on the Catholic side, and July 12, on the
Protestant side. At the St. Patrick's Day parade in Ottawa
in 1871, one of the speakers, Mr. W. H. Waller, as
reported in the *Irish Canadian* newspaper, emphasized the
equality that Roman Catholics enjoy in their "adopted
country. Here we have unlimited freedom, civil and religious equality, no special privileges existing for any class
of the population of which the other is disbarred, all being
equal under the constitution and before the laws." In
Thorold on the same day, the Reverend Father McEntee
"encouraged the members of the St. Patrick's Society by
exhorting them to unity and fidelity to their religion, and
never to be ashamed of religion or country." But an
account of the parade in Toronto suggests that while
liberty and equality existed officially, the reality for
Catholics was different.

The Toronto St. Patrick's Day parade receives several
full pages in the *Irish Canadian*. After printing the well-
known archbishop John Joseph Lynch's pastoral letter in
full, the newspaper goes on to describe the weather and
parade in detail, including a disruption of the procession
that occurred when a Protestant teamster who worked for

a contractor named Gearing deliberately tried to force his horses through the crowd. A young Catholic man struck him and was held back by parade marshals. The next morning, "when the Catholic laborers employed by Mr. Gearing in the erection of the Methodist church at McGill square came to work, as usual, they were told by Mr. Townsend, partner of Gearing there was nothing more for them to do there. In future no 'dogans' need apply, if they wished to escape being insulted or disembowelled." In the following issue, the "dogans" themselves wrote a letter confirming the story. They claimed a question was put to them when they arrived at work that morning: "What are you—a Roman Catholic or Protestant?" and when they replied that they were Roman Catholics, they were told they had to leave. "The foreman said an order had come down that morning directing the discharge of all the Roman Catholics engaged on the building."

While this is only one admittedly one-sided account of an incident, reading through nineteenth-century issues of *The Globe,* an openly anti-Catholic Toronto newspaper, gives a sense of the kind of anti-Catholic feelings that ran rampant, ebbing and flowing according to key events, at that time. On July 13, 1870, *The Daily Globe* describes the "Celebration of the Orange Anniversary in Toronto." Orange lodges from the countryside streamed into the city to join the procession. Speeches declared that "Orangeism was flourishing in Canada; that Orangemen had loyal hearts and that their watchword was 'No Surrender!' (loud applause)" A visitor from Scotland

declared that "he could have formed no conception
before he left home, of the numbers and position of the
Orangemen in Canada. . . . When he thought of the siege
of Derry, and the number of men who defended that city
. . . he thought in his heart, that Toronto could stand a
siege any time. (applause) He was quite sure if the Pope
had any Fenians to spare the Brethren of Toronto would
make short work of them." He then urged the "brethren"
to "Go on and conquer, and do not stop until you make
your kingdom the glory of the world."

The newspaper goes on to describe "incidents." A
Catholic driving a horse and carriage decked out in green
ribbons, like the Orange teamster at the St. Patrick's Day
parade, tried to interrupt the Orange procession. Stones
were thrown from the crowd, and the man was knocked
off his horse. Policemen intervened and "arrested the
carter." (This was a common pattern in these sectarian
incidents: provoked Catholics usually ended up being
arrested and then convicted by an Orange-influenced jury,
on the grounds that they had started it.) Later, some
"Young Britons" who had heard about the incident
marched down a Catholic street: "Silently, and with
scowling brows [the Catholics] watched the procession of
Young Britons, who filed past in perfect order, their band
playing a march." Stone-throwing and fights broke out,
and again the police "succeeded in restoring order, with
some difficulty."

The Reverend Dean Harris, in his history of the
Catholic Church in the Niagara Peninsula, written in

1895, tells a story about Father Grattan, priest of the parish of St. Catharines in the mid-1800s. Father Grattan believed that "there was a kindlier feeling existing between the two parties in the Old Country than in the New. 'I have known . . . the most intimate cordialities to exist between Catholics and Protestants in Ireland and doubts of one as to the ultimate salvation of the other have often seemed to me to mingle, in a strange sort of manner, the mirthful with the serious.'" Harris then relates the story of an Orange joke that circulated in Lincoln County, the area where the Smiths had settled: Last time Jerry Finnegan went to confession, he told a story of sin "as long as [his] arm." The priest asked him, "'Did you never do anything good at all since your last confession, Jerry?' 'Oh! Yes, your Reverence; I shot an Orangeman.' 'Thanks be to God,' replied the priest, heaving a sigh of relief; 'that wipes out all your other crimes.'"

When my mother and her brothers were growing up, the Niagara Peninsula was still largely Protestant. My uncle Neil remembers that there was always tension between the Catholics and Protestants. Since the nearest Catholic school was in the town of St. Catharines, too far to walk, my mother and uncles went to the public school close to their house. The schoolteacher boarded at a nearby house, until the school board found out she was boarding with Catholics. They made her move to a Protestant house, even though it was a much longer walk from the school.

When the school year was over, my mother and uncles went to Catholic summer school in St. Catharines for religion classes. On July 12, the festive marching band music of the Orange parade floated through the shady park across from the church. At lunchtime the Catholic kids made a break for it, tearing across the park to watch the parade. When Father Ryan discovered they were missing, he came after them, berating them for their betrayal. As I pieced together this history, I began to see my mother and grandmother's question about our friends as a vestige of this old animosity.

I TOOK A BUS out of Belfast to Cushendall, the town where the Dillons and Murrays, Hugh Dillon's parents on my mother's mother's side, came from. In Canada, Hugh Dillon married Anne Quinlivan, from County Clare. In the bright sunshine, I walked a mile out of town to a bed and breakfast. I dropped my pack on the doorstep and, drenched with sweat, rang the bell. Mary, the owner, bustled me inside, clucking sympathetically. "You'll be sunburnt. I can't stick the sun myself. Had you rung me up, I would have fetched you in the car and put your bag in the boot. Can I get you a wee cuppa?"

Mary told me about the rooms she had, listing the prices, which were double what I had been paying in hostels. "But I want to show you this one particular one. Now it's ten pounds, but if you don't like it, you just tell me," she said. She showed me up to what she called the attic, a beautiful sunny little room with a double bed, a sky-light window, and a television. Clean fluffy towels were folded neatly at the end of the bed. I wanted to kiss her. I had come down from the euphoria of my Donegal splurge and worried that my dwindling funds might mean I would have to cut my trip short.

Mary sat me at the kitchen table with tea, sandwiches, cookies, and buttered raisin bread. When she found out I was travelling alone, she told me stories about single women getting picked up by strangers, raped, and murdered. But after I promised I wouldn't take any rides from strangers, she told me how to find the Catholic cemetery and the parish priest.

I walked about two and a half miles up the road to the cemetery. It was on a rise of land that overlooked the green plaid hills of Antrim. The grass in the graveyard was lush and slightly overgrown. Pink roses and deep green ivy climbed the fence. The older graves were adorned with weathered grey stone Celtic crosses, the four arms of the cross enclosed by a circle. The crosses were carved with the intricate looping patterns of Celtic designs, showing the melding of the old spirituality with Christianity. I saw Murrays here, but no Dillons. But a man in a hardware store in Cushendall had told me there were Dillons in the town of Dunloy, not far away. So I guessed that Catherine Murray was probably from Cushendall and her husband, John Dillon, from nearby.

I found one gravestone that could have been a relative. It was of Alexander Murray, who died in 1891. His daughter Catherine, the stone said, died in Cleveland, Ohio, in 1888.

The names Alexander and Catherine echo through the
generations in Hugh Dillon's family. He named his first-
born child Alexander and his eighth-born Catherine,
presumably after his mother. So this Alexander could have
been a cousin on his mother's side. He could even have been
a very long-lived brother of Catherine. This was probably
a long shot, Murray being a name almost as common as
Smith in Ireland, but I found myself growing desperate to
make some concrete connection with this place. Some of
my ancestors' bones were probably lying beneath my feet
in this cemetery. I wondered if any ghosts haunted this
place, and if they did, would they recognize me?

At the Catholic priest's residence, I waited for him to
return from a golf game. When he did, he led me into the
large dining room and invited me to wait while he looked
for the church records. But when he returned, we quickly
figured out that my family went back further than the
records. He explained to me that during the era of the
Penal Laws, record-keeping became extremely difficult.
Some parishes had no permanent churches.

"And you have to remember," he said gently, "not all
families wanted to maintain connections with their relatives who emigrated. There was considerable bitterness
over land, you see." His tight-lipped smile made me
wonder about the bitterness he might be harbouring
himself over some old family grievance.

My great-great-grandfather Hugh Dillon left the land
of his birth in 1840, when he was about twenty. He
earned his living as a cooper, a builder and repairer of

wooden barrels and tubs. With a trade, he wasn't the poorest of the Irish. The worst potato crop failures didn't hit till 1845. So what led him to leave behind the land where the bones of generations of ancestors lay, probably knowing he would never find a way to return? Even Robert Whyte, who left in the midst of the worst throes of the famine, writes in his *Journey of an Irish Coffin Ship:* "Many and deep are the wounds that the sensitive heart inflicts upon its possessor, as he journeys through life's pilgrimage, but on few occasions are they so acutely felt as when one is about to part from those who formed a portion of his existence; deeper still pierces the pang as the idea presents itself that the separation may be forever. . . . It was a charming morning on which I left dear old Ireland. . . . It was a morning calculated to inspire the drooping soul with hope auguring future happiness. Too soon I arrived at the quay and left my last footprint on my native land." And Gerald Keegan, in his *Famine Diary*, writes: "Passing close to the shore we had a view of the coast from Ardmore to Cape Clear. Aileen sat with me all day, our eyes fixed on the land we loved. Knowing, as it swept past us, it was the last time we would ever gaze upon it, our hearts were too full for speech. Towards evening, the ship drew away from it, until the hills of Kerry became so faint that they could hardly be distinguished from the clouds that hovered over them. When I finally turned away my eyes from where I knew the dear old land was, my heart throbbed as if it would burst. Farewell, Erin."

But even before the famine, life was hard in Ireland. Early nineteenth-century visitors to the country describe the poverty as the worst in Europe. Gustave de Beaumont, a French traveller, wrote: "I have seen the Indian in his forests, and the Negro in his chains, and thought, as I contemplated their pitiable condition, that I saw the very extreme of human wretchedness; but I did not then know the condition of unfortunate Ireland." An 1841 census indicates that more than half the rural population lived in the lowest class of house, a windowless single-room mud cabin. Their pigs, if they had any, lived in the same house. Stones served as chairs, and beds and blankets were a rare luxury. Potatoes and water had come to be the principal diet of the Irish. Cecil Woodham-Smith, in his book *The Great Hunger,* explains that "all this wretchedness and misery could, almost without exception, be traced to a single source—the system under which land had come to be occupied and owned in Ireland, a system produced by centuries of successive conquests, rebellions, confiscations and punitive legislation."

Large estates that had once belonged to distinguished and ancient Irish families were dismantled under the paranoia and greed of the Penal Laws of the eighteenth century. Not only were Catholic estates divided under these laws, but Catholics were forbidden to purchase land. Gradually, formerly prosperous families were reduced to landless peasants, leasing land that had once been theirs from absentee English landlords. As Woodham-Smith says, "Until the famine, it was by no means uncommon for poor peasants in mud cabins to make wills bequeathing estates which had long ago been confiscated from their forefathers." Middlemen were hired to do the absentee landlords' dirty work, since the landlords for the most part found Ireland an unpleasant and hostile place to live. The middleman's job was to lever as much money out of the estate as possible. The law was on his side. The Irish were forced to pay rent on small parcels of land that could barely support their families. Without capital, they had to find a way to build homes for their families and pay their rent. The tenants were in a state of perpetual debt to their landlords, and they had to live with the constant threat of eviction. Any money they might earn from their crops had to go to the landlord, instead of to improving life for their families. No wonder the Irish subsisted on potatoes. They were slaves on their own land, caught in a vicious cycle of debt and poverty. And because they were Catholic, they were outlaws, enemies to the government. They could expect no earth-shattering change in their situation from that front.

The notes my mother had collected about our family contained a rare specific detail: that Hugh Dillon had sailed for the new world from Belfast on Easter Sunday morning, 1840, with his brother James and his cousin Alexander Darragh. All through the years that these scribbled notes had been passed on and recopied from mother and father to daughter and son, this little notation had survived, a typically Catholic cherishing of a magical, auspicious date. On Easter, a time of resurrections and new beginnings, the breeze off Belfast carried hope for Hugh and his family. If he was not feeling sick from the sea swells, he could have stood on the deck and watched the northern coast of Ireland and the island of Rathlin disappearing behind him.

That day, Hugh became a voyager in a long line of Irish voyagers. As a Catholic, he would have known the famous story of St. Brendan, another voyager. In the sixth century A.D., Brendan travelled for seven years on the North Atlantic with his brother monks in a curragh made of a light wooden frame covered with ox hides and smeared with fat. They spent Holy Saturday on an island thick with white sheep the size of cows, and on Easter Sunday, they built their cooking fire on the back of a giant whale. Each year for the seven years they were at sea, the wind and waves buffeted their little craft back to the same islands to celebrate Easter in a preordained place. After seven years, they were blown ashore on the Promised Land of the Saints, a place where night didn't fall and day never ended. Barrind, the monk who had first sparked Brendan's imagination with the story of the Promised Land of the Saints, said, "Do you not perceive from the fragrance of our clothing that we have been in God's paradise?"

Over the years since the account of Brendan's voyage first appeared in print, scholars have theorized about the location of the paradise that Brendan describes. On maps and globes between the thirteenth and sixteenth centuries, Brendan's islands appeared in various places out in the

Atlantic Ocean. Some placed the islands near Iceland, others just east of Newfoundland. A popularly held theory was that the Promised Land of the Saints was really North America, and that the Irish were the first Europeans to reach that continent, where, if you're far enough north in the summer, the day does never end. In the 1970s, a British navigation scholar named Tim Severin crossed the Atlantic in a craft he had built copying Brendan's description, proving that it could have been done, especially given the Irish skill and familiarity with sea voyages.

As Hugh slept with his brother and cousin in the cramped quarters of an Irish ship and the waves of the Atlantic grew into a relentless rhythm, did he dream of forest-scented clothes and days that went on forever?

IT SEEMS TO ME that in Ireland, you choose your mythology, knowing full well that it is a biased story in a history of biased stories, Catholic or Protestant, based on love and passion for what you believe in, not on reason and fact alone. I don't believe it's possible to separate myth from reality in Irish history, since the two are so intertwined. I knew that in trying to imagine the story of my ancestors' migration to Canada, I was creating my own myth. My ancestors as underdogs was an image I could sink my teeth into: the Orange status quo–loving bad guys, trying to keep Ontario Protestant; the tenacious, long-suffering Catholics holding fast to their "superstitions," no matter the cost.

My great-grandparents were probably not ardent Irish nationalists, because if they had been, more stories of it would have survived. I don't know if they suffered the humiliating sting of real religious persecution—being hindered in finding work or housing, for instance. Most of them were farmers. But my uncles remember they were proud of being Irish and prouder of being Catholic. I imagine them digging in their Catholic heels, loving their Catholic faith more than ever for having to suffer silently and subtly for it.

I thought that now I could better understand my mother's disappointment and frustration as some of her kids got divorced, stopped going to Confession, and finally stopped going to Mass altogether. Two of my sisters started going to the Anglican Church, at least sporadically, after they got married, joking that it was "Catholic lite: all the ceremony, half the guilt." I saw my rejection of Catholicism as a teenager in a different light now too. I wondered if it was more about conforming than I had realized. Did it just become too embarrassing to be Catholic? I remember the jokes about the rhythm method, big Catholic families, hypocritical attitudes about premarital sex and Confession. I wanted to be seen as reasonable, logical, and intelligent, not as a superstitious hypocrite.

If there was any truth to my Catholic underdog myth, I thought its legacy came to me and my siblings in a complicated dance of pride and embarrassment.

9.
Giant's Causeway

As life becomes more orderly, more deliberate, the supernatural world sinks further away.

—W. B. Yeats, *Irish Folklore, Legend and Myth*

In the holiday town of Portstewart, on the north coast, it had been lashing down rain since I arrived. I'd had a day of travelling on buses, and now a thin headache was pressing behind my eyes. But the hostel was warm and comfortable, with a good fire burning and music playing in the sitting room, so I sat and read Yeats and studied my Lonely Planet guidebook. In the evening, the rain stopped. I walked out to the cliff that overlooked the busy seaside strip through town on one side and the wild sweep of sea on the other. Someone had set shabby brown armchairs out in the grass on the cliff facing the sea and the sunset. The sun was setting now, spreading an orange glow over the shops of the town, the grass of the cliff, and the deep brown chairs nestled there like rock formations. I identified with a kind of paradox in the chairs: turning your back on the obligations of the world to face the uncomplicated beauty of the sun going down over the water, but taking your comfortable chair with you.

The next morning, I woke up with a fierce head cold. The hostel experience was wearing thin. I was in a skinny bunk bed in a shared room with no bedside table, no reading light, and no central heating. I longed for the comfort of a good double bed, piled high with blankets and flanked by Kleenex boxes and hot tea. In the hostel kitchen, making my toast and tea among strangers, I felt a thick fog swaddling my mind. Voices echoed down the long hall of my blocked ear passages. Una, an American, one of the women sharing my room, stood at the counter sipping her coffee, a turquoise-and-pink mohair shawl draped over her arm.

"Are you catching the bus to the Giant's Causeway?" she asked.

"Yes, I am," I answered, or thought I did anyway, since I could barely hear my own voice in my throbbing head.

She pulled up a chair beside me. "It sounds like a powerful spot. Do you know the legend about Finn MacCool? He's supposed to have built this highway of rock to cross the sea to a woman he loved in Scotland."

When we boarded the bus, Una sat in the seat beside me. As she talked, I nodded and tried to be discreet about blowing my nose. Every time I turned towards the window and blew, I'd have a few moments of clarity where I could focus on what she was telling me. The rest of the time, her words swirled in a heady haze of fragments: "the triple goddess," "my process," "empowering." Una was not her birthname but a name she'd adopted to signal a fresh start; it was Celtic for "the white one," meaning the moon. She'd taken a leave of absence from work to make this trip; she was concentrating especially on the goddess sites.

By the time the bus reached the path down to the Giant's Causeway, I felt completely disoriented by the intimate snippets of a stranger's life swimming through my clouded consciousness. My passivity was turning to active irritation as Una and I made our way down the path to the causeway and her personal revelations continued to spill forth. Had she asked, I would have told her that I had come to the Giant's Causeway mostly because my grandmother's grandfather and his family came from this area. I wanted to walk in peace along cliffs that had, in part, given birth to the myths that had shaped their lives. A cool wind blew a fine sea mist across our path, but the clouds were white and broken; I thought the sky might clear and make perfect walking weather. I restrained myself from breaking into a run.

As we approached the hexagonal columns of basalt that make up the Giant's Causeway, Una emitted a disappointed bleat. "Oh! I thought they would be a lot bigger than that!" she said. "This is a World Heritage Site, did you know that? I mean, I was expecting something really stunning."

A young Irish man standing nearby flashed her a look of irritation. I was irritated myself at the noise of someone else's impressions crashing in before my own had even formed. I walked a few steps down the rocks.

"This doesn't look that giant to me," Una said, following me as she fished her camera out of her bag.

The Irish man behind her couldn't contain himself any longer. "Sorry to disappoint you," he said. "Maybe we should've had it built into a theme park for the tourists."

Una glanced at him sideways, then concentrated on snapping some photos. "Could you take my picture?" she asked me. As Una posed, I wondered about the ugly (North) American syndrome. Are North Americans more obsessed with order and control than other cultures? We want experience, like our movies and our food, neatly packaged and immediately accessible; we seem to have an especially hard time appreciating subtlety and the hard work of building understanding bit by bit, even the spiritual understanding that Una claimed to be after. I handed Una back her camera and politely made my escape.

Out of sight of the crowd, I perched on one of the "chairs" formed by the rock columns. The rocks are flat hexagon shapes, about the size of a large plate, with smoothed out depressions where sea water collects. The day I was there, the grey sky and dampness made the rock appear almost black. The tightly packed rock also extends underground, or thrusts up out of the sea in narrow columns. Science explains that the phenomenon occurred because of a volcanic eruption. The lava solidified into columns, some as high as forty feet. But like so many geological features in Ireland, this one has both a scientific explanation and a mythological one. In her book *Gods and Heroes of the Celts,* Marie-Louise Sjoestedt says, "Some peoples, such as the Romans, think of their myths historically; the Irish think of their history mythologically; and so, too, of their geography."

The giant of the Giant's Causeway story is Fionn mac Cumhaill (Finn MacCool), who lived in the third century, when thick woods still covered Ireland and wolves and deer still ran wild. Finn's birthname was Demne. His mother, Murna, fearing her husband's enemies, sent Demne to live in secret in the woods with two wise women. The women taught him to hunt and fish so well that he could outrun rabbits and catch deer without the help of a dog. He learned to remove a thorn from his heel at full flight through the woods. He could leap a hurdle as high as his forehead and run full speed under a hurdle as low as his knees. One day, the boy was wandering the woods when he came upon a mansion where the sons of Irish chiefs were trained to be men. Demne was invited to join a game of hurling, but his team kept winning easily. To even up the competition, his team members were subtracted one by one until Demne won the game single-handedly. The other boys were jealous of his strength, and so he left them. But they admired his fine, well-proportioned body and called him Finn, meaning "fair."

The wise women sent Finn to learn the art of poetry from the bard Finegas, who lived by the river Boyne. A prophecy told that Finegas would catch and eat the Salmon of Knowledge that swam the river. When he finally caught the salmon, he brought it to Finn and asked him to cook it, warning him not to eat any of it. But when Finn brought the roasted salmon to Finegas, Finegas asked, "Did you eat any?" and Finn replied, "No, but I burnt my thumb while cooking it, and I stuck my thumb in my mouth to cool it." Finegas was silent for a moment as he realized the prophecy had been fulfilled. "Take the rest of the salmon and eat it, Fionn mac Cumhaill. The prophecy has come not to me, but to you."

The knowledge from the salmon, the ways of the wild, hunting, poetry, and magic helped Finn grow into a loved and respected leader of the Fiana, or Fenians, a powerful warrior society that roamed freely between the world of humans and the spirit world. The Fiana lived outside of ordinary Irish society, clanless, without the protection of the law. They were semi-nomadic, dwelling on the margins, beyond human responsibility, slipping in and out of the depths of the woods and the fairy domain of the *sidhe,* shifting shape to become human, deer, or dog. But they were not seen as outlaws; in fact, the Fenians took on the role of protecting Ireland from foreign invasions, both human and fairy, and their eccentricities were expected. The Irish recognized that no one tethered to the everyday, orderly world of human society could achieve the magical feats that these men (and women) could. Who had time to walk across the North Channel when you were busy cutting peat and digging potatoes?

A promising path of blue had cleared in the sky, so I set off on my walk along the cliff. This walk is part of the Ulster Way, a system of walking paths that twists through Northern Ireland and stretches past Cushendall, where Hugh Dillon and his parents came from. After I had walked a short distance, I was alone, looking down on the sea foaming into the strange rock shapes below the cliff. I thought about the giant, Fionn mac Cumhaill, and my ancestors, whose view of the world was so different from mine that Fionn could live in it alongside them. As my relatives collected seaweed from the beaches to fertilize their crops, they could look out at the basalt steps that Fionn's magic raised up out of the sea, and they could know that things were at work in the world that were larger than their own lives. Yeats says that Fionn and his ilk were thought of as giants because their actions were larger than life. They were beings sprung from people with imaginations like children, who accepted that mystery and magic existed beyond the everyday world of humans. I felt a long way off from my ancestors' experience of the world. For them, the landscape was such a constant it became embedded with a mythology that stretched for generations.

The cool, moist wind had a clearing effect on my nasal passages; the fresh sea air was dissipating the fog that had

immobilized me on the bus. Green fields sloped gently up
from the cliff. The path followed closely along the cliff
edge and occasionally veered inland through a field,
where I had to climb the steps of wooden stiles to get over
fences. A huge, shiny purple-black raven hopped in the
grass along the path. When he saw me, he hopped into my
path, teasing me with his beady black eyes. His hook beak
opened wide, but no sound came out. Ravens, in mytholo-
gies from the Pacific Northwest to Ireland, have a reputation for being able to travel between the land of the living
and the land of the dead. He nosed his open beak at me as
if trying to whisper something I couldn't understand. His
canny eyes seemed to mock my puny intuition: "Come on,
human, do I have to spell it out for you?"

After a while, the sun came out in full force. Thinking
had left me. I was all draining sinuses, streaming eyes,
strong legs pumping a walking rhythm. Clarity overwhelmed me: blue sky, black cliff, green grass. And no one
else around. I lay down on the grassy edge of the cliff to
savour it. Though it was still too cool to take off my
sweater or jacket, the sun felt deliciously warm on my face.
With my head at the very edge of the cliff, and my body
anchoring me to land, I tipped back my chin: sea and sky
were reversed. I tried to find a horizon. Slowly, I became
aware of a familiarity seeping into me, rushing through my
bones like warmth, a feeling that I knew this place. A
beach of black rock speckled with shell appeared before
me, stretching in towards a low, grassy cliff. A little girl in
a black woollen coat made her way up the beach towards

a white cottage. I saw her, but I also was her, watching my own small feet moving up the black beach.

I tried to poise myself on the brink of this "vision," expectant, waiting to see more. But this was all I saw, and it, and the rush of familiarity, disappeared. I sat up and looked around to see if anyone had been watching me. As I sat up, my sinuses drained and cleared my head again with a snap. I tried to anchor myself to some rational explanation for what had just happened. Had I fallen into a thirty-second power nap? Had I seen some movie with this scene in it, and the setting here had evoked a memory of it?

When we were kids, my sisters and brother and I sometimes played burying games. When it was my turn to be victim, as the leaves or snow gradually covered my body, then my head, ears, face, I slipped into some kind of altered state—the voices became farther away; I heard them, but I couldn't respond to them. What they were saying didn't quite register. I entered some other realm, where time didn't pass and bodily sensation ceased. When my sisters clawed the snow from my ears and pulled me up, I snapped back to reality as if waking up. The world looked brighter for a few minutes then. I noticed the tufts of snow balanced in lines along the polished bare branches of a cherry tree, the tangy smell of the snow—the same smell we carried into the house on our mittens—and my little brother's laugh that ran up and down a scale like a song. Everything seemed strange and wonderful for those few minutes.

As an adult, it still happens, though I have less opportunity to be buried these days. It's a delicate thing—I can't will it, but I need to surrender to it or be taken by surprise. Suspending consciousness is how I think of it. Any time I've tried to make it happen on purpose, I've failed.

Even before I left on my trip to Ireland, even as I planned the places I would go, I held in my heart a romantic little fantasy that I would set foot on Irish soil and suddenly feel that I'd come home; ghosts would talk to me in graveyards, and old codgers in tiny Irish villages would tell me I looked just like someone they'd once known and I'd discover that I could play the harp and sing in Irish. But here I was when I least expected it, when I'd already settled comfortably into the idea of being a foreigner, and I'd been startled by a tap of recognition. Maybe some door had opened momentarily, and the past had reached through and nudged me. If the water's edge was a place where doorways opened between worlds, what world had I glimpsed in this little girl walking thoughtfully up the beach? Her clothes were from an era that didn't go back far enough to make her Hugh's mother. The clothes reminded me of a photograph I had of my mother as a girl, in a bulky cloth coat and sturdy little lace-up boots. But why in this place? And can a place really harbour human memories?

ON THE SOUTH END of a small Gulf Island in British Columbia, a sheltered sandy bay catches the sun, and the tide scoops smooth pockets out of the sandstone rock shaded by fragrant cedar and shiny, red-barked arbutus trees. A swinging rope dangles invitingly from one of the arbutus trees, as it has since my husband was a teenager and, with his sister and brother, spent hot afternoons catapulting off the end of the rope and into the Strait of Georgia. David's ancestors, the Kwakwaka'wakw, didn't occupy this island, but they were close by, living a life of abundance harvested from these same waters: salmon, cockles, clams, oysters, sea lions, oolichans, herring roe, seaweed. The first time David took me to the island, he showed me the midden, which was easiest to see on a shelf of land near the beach, where the earth had been dug out to build a church. The church had been abandoned long ago, but we could see a cutaway of about five feet of bleached white shell, packed flatly like layers of noodle in a casserole. David said the midden probably extended another fifteen feet underground. He had scooped buckets of it out with a front-end loader once, to use as fill for fencepost holes.

"What's it from? The tide bringing in shells?" I asked.

"It's from people eating shellfish. Harvesting it. You know, sucking the meat out and tossing the shell? Year after year, in this same place. That's how long they lived here."

I was unable to speak for a minute. I'd never seen such a physical representation of the long line of human attachment to a piece of land. David told me that longhouses had occupied the bay for hundreds, probably thousands, of years. The southwest exposure, the large protected bay that drains out almost completely at low tide to make gathering shellfish easy, and the shallower water, perfect for swimming, offered everything that humans would look for in a place to live. Natural freshwater springs gurgled into a small stream that drained into the bay. On warm summer nights, with the moon hanging over the bay, the slurp of the tide going out, and the quiet pop and bubble of shellfish hiding themselves in the sand, the people came out of their longhouses and built a small driftwood fire up on the beach to steam the shellfish open. Kids up to their thighs in the sun-warmed bay swept their hands through the water, creating streaks of glowing green phosphorescence like comet trails. They splashed the water into the air and sent showers of green light sprinkling down. Around the fire, with the smell of the ocean and cedars on the breeze, the people sat steeped in gratitude for the salty, smoky taste of clams and oysters and the beauty of this place.

One spring, when David and I were living in the Fraser valley, David arranged for me to have a couple of weeks away from home in a secluded place where I could write. The place was an empty cabin on the hundred-acre farm that now occupies the south end of the island, the farm where David had spent his high-school years, and that he had returned to as a caretaker in his twenties.

When the island was made into a reservation in 1916, the south end was left out of it. A mission run by the North American Society for the Propagation of the Gospel stood on the site. Here the missionaries had easy access to a host of people who had been alienated from their land and traditions. But there was a lot more history there that I learned only much later. The farm changed hands over the years until the current owner bought it, as a weekend and summer place for himself and his family. David's step-father, Paul, a gruff but kind-hearted man who left behind a brutal past when he escaped from Czechoslovakia in the sixties, became the full-time caretaker of the property, living in his own little cabin on a ten-acre plot of land. The rest of the island is Indian reserve, lush and over-grown, with some remnants of old-growth forest, but largely second-growth cedars and fir and lots of berries. At the north end is a small village, a cluster of houses, a ferry terminal, the band office, and the elementary school. The occasional kayaker visits the island, but other than that, there are no tourists, because there is nowhere for them to go.

David and I drove over in my 1965 Valiant. The road from the ferry terminal to the farm winds through bush for three long miles of mud trenches that you don't want to let your wheels slide into because you won't get back out again. You straddle the ruts, circle the washouts, and when the puddles are too deep and wide to go around, you cross your fingers, pray the engine doesn't stall, and drive straight through.

David's friend from the village, Richard, who worked on the farm when they needed him, helped us unload the car. He had moved to the island from California when he married his wife, Marie. Richard and Marie and their kids had been good friends to David when he was caretaker of the farm. Richard was a kind, soft-spoken man who liked to laugh. He didn't seem to see anything odd about my desire to spend two weeks alone in a one-room cabin with no electricity or running water. He promised to haul me in a load of firewood in the back of the farm truck to stoke up the Super Chalet woodstove.

"You'll probably need it," he said. "Get the dampness out of the place."

I swept the fine black grit out of the cabin, the leavings of bugs chewing their way through the roofing, while David and Richard climbed up and put tarps over the leaky roof. I moved the writing desk in front of a window that looked down over the slope of hay meadows, the graveyard, and the beach beyond.

That night, the rain started, tap dancing steadily on the plastic tarp on the roof. The Coleman lantern hissed from its hook on the rafter, but it was better than the kerosene lamp, which leaked a stream of smelly black smoke and barely threw enough light. When I looked outside, I could only see shapes: a bulk of black that was the woods, a stretch of paler black that was the meadow. I put on my rubber boots and slipped out into the rainy night to the outhouse, which was a lot more "out" than "house," a little wood platform propped between two trees. For such a quiet place, it sure was noisy. Everything was water— dripping, tapping, spattering, rushing. Beneath the dominant sound of the rain, a hundred other tiny noises were alive and moving in the dark around me. I thought I could hear the ocean surging up against the rocks on the shore and pulling back. The tide seemed to pull at me, too, to go down to the water.

During the day in the fine, steady rain, I hacked away at the overgrown blackberry bushes in front of the cabin or planted lettuce seedlings in the mud of the garden to earn my keep at the farm. But the beach beckoned me like a whispering voice, like an old person, hands on hips, waiting for me. In my rubber boots and rain cape, I sloshed down the hill, through the wet grass to the grave-yard I could see from my window. If I had to be dead, I would want to be in a place like this: the graves were enclosed by a simple wire-and-post fence; it was a quiet, green place overlooking the beach and perfumed with plump purple lilacs in bloom. I sat on the smooth rocks below the dripping arbutus trees and watched the ocean pitted with rain. But in spite of the beauty of this paradise, I was overtaken by an uneasiness that I couldn't shake. I had the tingling-hair-on-the-back-of-the-neck feeling that I was being watched. A little later, I saw Paul, out of hearing range, standing under some trees smoking and looking out at the bay. He didn't see me.

Each day I went down to the water and the unsettled feeling I had grew. Some nights, after staring out at the pale moonlight on the meadow and graveyard, wanting to go down to the beach, I walked over to Paul's cabin instead and shared his pre-bedtime cocktail of vodka and cold coffee. He washed down a few painkillers to numb the ache of his arthritis, told me some stories about when

David was a boy, then snapped into a sudden rage about
the farm and the way things were done, or weren't done.
I thanked him for the vodka and made my way back
through the woods to my cabin. I bumped around in the
dark with my flashlight, looking for candles, not wanting
to light the Coleman lamp and drown out the song of the
crickets and frogs. I wasn't afraid to be alone in the cabin:
Paul's place wasn't far and there was a telephone down at
the main house. I put my uneasiness down to loneliness
and the unfamiliarity of the place.

One day I walked down to the ferry and went over to
Chemainus to do some shopping. I saw a telephone booth
and thought I could catch David at home. When he asked
me how I was doing, I told him, "It's beautiful, but . . ."

"But what?"

"It's just this weird uneasiness I have here." I tried to
explain my feelings to him.

When I was done, he said, "I'm not really surprised.
I've heard other people mention that kind of thing before.
The guy who built the cabin you're in used to have dreams
about the island. I didn't mention it before, but apparently
some bad things happened there many years ago."

"Bad things like what?"

"I heard a story about a battle between the British navy
and the aboriginal people who lived in the village on the
south end. The village was destroyed." That was about all
David knew of the story at the time. "They had some
cleansing ceremonies down at the beach a few years ago.
So you're not the only one who's felt it."

On the ferry trip back to the island, some girls on their way home from school teased me about my long walk to the farm.

"You can ride in the school bus with us to the turnoff," they offered.

I took them up on it. "We can walk with you part of the way," the oldest girl said as the bus swung along the mud road. "But we can't go past the dump because of the wild dogs."

Four girls accompanied me up the road towards the farm. As we approached the dump, we could hear the noisy cawing of crows.

"You better be careful," said the oldest girl as they stopped short on the road. "We don't go to the south end because of those wild dogs. People get attacked."

I thanked them for walking with me and hurried past the dump on my own, keeping an ear open for the scrabble of clawed feet coming up behind me. Maybe there were wild dogs on the island. Or maybe parents were just trying to keep their kids from wandering over to the south end, where the people were strangers and unpredictable, and where bad things had happened in the past.

On the walk back to the cabin, I tried to put a name to whatever I had felt down at the beach. I wondered if Paul felt it too, standing on the rocks day after day, looking out at the bay. You know you're in a paradise; you should feel incredibly light and blessed, but instead a sadness oppresses you. Sadness: that's as close as I could come to identifying it. The idea that the land could retain emotions from our human past seemed appealing but far-fetched. It seemed even more far-fetched to think that I would recognize the sadness myself. Then I felt flattered that David would think I had some kind of spooky psychic ability. Then I doubted myself altogether: it was probably coincidence.

When I got home to the Fraser valley, I asked Inger what she thought of the idea. Inger was the reiki master whose house we shared and looked after when she travelled. She said, "You'd have to be a brick not to pick up on that kind of negative energy." At the time, I laughed and again felt that tingle of pleasure at the possibility that I might have this unexpected capacity. But as a reiki master, Inger, like the giants of Finn MacCool's time, dwelt on the fringes herself; the realm of the Otherworld seemed quite real to her in a way that it didn't to me.

David took a more scientific approach. To him, there was nothing spooky about it. "There's science behind it," he said. "A beach, or any water's edge, is transitional, a riparian area. I learned about it in geography. Scientists know that it's a special world—not water, but not land either. Unique species live in those areas. So it would make sense that the same thing holds true for the non-physical world."

It wasn't until recently that I learned the details of what really happened on Kuper Island. A woman in the Penelakut band office confirmed that the story about the gunboat firing on the village on the south end of the island was true. The people were called the Lamalcha, and they were not originally part of the Penelakut band. She told me that a recent book, called *The Terror of the Coast,* explained the whole story in detail. The author, Chris Arnett, used oral history from local elders, as well as British naval and other government records, to reconstruct an astonishing narrative. The story goes that in the mid-1800s, the Lamalcha people, who lived on the idyllic south end of Kuper Island, were known for being uncooperative with the British government on land deals. They wanted to hold on to not only their land, but also their control of it. Contrary to what I always thought, the Lamalcha and other West Coast indigenous peoples did have a very precise system of land tenure, which involved privileges for using the land for food and other purposes. Certain families had rights to particular parcels of land. No one else would be allowed to use that land or live on it without permission from that family. The government's attempt to make land treaties with the Cowichan, Halalt, Penelakut, Chemainus, and Lamalcha people failed repeatedly because, as Arnett says, the aboriginal people "would not sell their people's land at any price."

In the spring of 1863, four white settlers were murdered in the southern Gulf Islands: two "transient" men who were camped on a small island, and a father and daughter, camped on another island. Partly because of the Lamalchas' reputation for resistance, the British centred their efforts to capture the criminals on the village of Lamalcha, the same spot where David had shown me the thick midden. On April 20, a British gunboat, the

Forward, anchored in front of the village. "Seven or eight large houses stood along the beach inside a small crescent-shaped bay enclosed on both sides by thickly-forested points of land. . . . The large-scale migrations to procure food resources had yet to begin and most, if not all, of the families were present. As a result, the village had its full complement of warriors." The British demanded that the criminals be turned over to them. The oral history that Arnett collected supports the story that David heard when he lived on Kuper: that the murderers were not surrendered to the British because they weren't there.

In spite of a massive display of firepower, the British had to retreat from Kuper Island on this first foray, having been repelled by a small but strategic force of Lamalcha warriors. Humiliated by his defeat, the commander, Lascelles, returned to Lamalcha on May 2, this time with two ships, the *Forward* and the *Grappler*. "Seeing that the village was deserted except for 'a large number of dogs,' Lascelles allowed a small landing party . . . to go ashore and 'set fire to the Indian village.'" They destroyed some canoes and the seven lodges, which would have held a population of about one hundred people. The British then pronounced the place "completely destroyed."

The petulant frenzy of this last violence and the words "completely destroyed" had a sudden effect on me. What arrogance the British had to think that their guns had the power to wipe out what had been standing for generations. Suddenly it made sense to me that what stood there was more than just a few buildings and fortifications. This was a place where families had lived and died, played and loved; they had named it and knew it intimately. Their mythology, their art, their language, reflected the creatures they saw in the ocean, the shapes of water sculpting stone, the constant music of water dripping from trees, lapping the shore. Suddenly the idea that the land held ghosts and memories seemed not only possible, but glaringly obvious.

Sometimes in a quiet place, where for a few minutes we lose our grip on the ordered world we are so sure of, something is revealed, just enough to tell us we are only murmurs in a din of voices occupying this place down through the years. But when we are alienated from the land of our ancestors, whether by force or by choice, what happens to those voices? Who is there to hear them?

When my mother died, she had been living in British Columbia for several years. She liked the mild weather, the almost year-round gardening, but it never became her home the way the Niagara Peninsula had been. So we decided to bury her in the graveyard in Ontario, near her mother's and father's graves, on land where our immigrant history, at least, ran for a few hundred years. When I went to her grave on my last visit, I felt glad she was at home. But I walked away with an incredible loneliness, as I realized how detached I had become from our past. The land we had grown up on was no longer ours; the Catholic past my mother had maintained no longer felt like my own either. What was I moving towards to take their place?

10.

SKELLIG MICHAEL

A hedge of trees surrounds me, a blackbird's lay sings to me,
praise I shall not conceal,
Above my lined book the trilling of the birds sings to me.
A clear-voiced cuckoo sings to me in a gray cloak from the tops of the
bushes
May the Lord save me from Judgment; well do I write under the
greenwood.

—WRITTEN BY A NINTH-CENTURY IRISH MONK IN THE MARGIN OF
A MANUSCRIPT, "THE SCRIBE IN THE WOODS"

I HAD FOLLOWED MOST of the place names pencilled in
on my mother's chart, worried that I would run out of
time. With about a week left, I decided to take a detour
down to County Kerry to see the skelligs Denise had told
me about back in Clare. She had also raved about a good
hostel in Cahirciveen, and since the weather had taken a
rare summery turn, I was in a holiday mood.

On the west coast, it was surreally sunny and very
hot—the hottest, I was told, it had been in seven years.

My room in the hostel had only two beds, no roommate, and a window that opened out onto a view of dark blue mountain with a white church below it and hundreds of white birds wheeling in the sky. Travellers gathered to chat in the kitchen, thanks mostly to the efforts of a sociable young American named Jeff, who was spending his summer working as a jack of all trades in the hostel. He introduced all the guests to each other, with a few notes of interest like where we were from or the kind of work we did. Jeff was eighteen and had a new Celtic tattoo he'd had done in Ireland. He was working on his Irish accent and had incorporated a few Irish-isms into his speech, like "brilliant," "half-six" (instead of six-thirty), and "cracking." His enthusiasm for things Irish was infectious.

On my first evening, I met Akiko, a Japanese woman, compact and ready for anything in an oversized T-shirt, walking shorts, and bright new running shoes. Akiko radiated independence and a sneaky sense of humour. We discovered we were living parallel lives on opposite sides of the world. We were both the same age, both writers, and both had younger partners named David. Our mothers had both died of cancer. As Akiko poured some tea for me on the balcony at the hostel, she leaned over my shoulder to look at the book I was reading: Yeats's *Writing on Irish Folklore, Legend and Myth*. She showed me hers: the same book, in Japanese.

Under the influence of the unusual heat, Akiko, Jeff, and I fell into a lazy holiday routine. We ate a leisurely breakfast on the hostel balcony, sharing stories of our lives back home, then Akiko and I did some shopping and walking while Jeff looked after his hostel duties. Then we met up with Jeff's friend Max, an older man from the village, and drove out to the beach, a place as idyllic as its name, which was something like the Blue Strand. The water was breathtakingly cold. Jeff swam anyway, the only person at the beach fully submerged, while Akiko and I waded, and Max stood fully clothed, smoking.

One warm evening, I asked Akiko if she'd like to go for a walk to look for some ruins and stone forts. We set out, she in her bright white running shoes and I in my scuffed boots. When I had led us into a bog of black mud that squeezed up through the seams of our shoes, within sight of the ruins but still a swamp-crossing away, Akiko confessed that she'd misunderstood my English and thought we were going to look in the stores. But she good-naturedly rinsed her white runners in the river and we went on. When we reached the ruins, we sat beneath the crumbling stone walls, with the sun turning orange.

"My David does the sweat lodge in Belgium," Akiko said as she scraped mud off her shoes with a stone. (We had taken to calling our partners "my" and "your" David.)

"Oh!" I exclaimed.

"The Indian sweat lodge," she explained. "Do you know it?"

"Yes," I said. "They have sweat lodges in Belgium?"

"Many people practise it there. It's very popular. I have been in it two times. And your David and you?"

"Yes," I said. More was required of me, but I wasn't sure what else to say.

I thought of Helmut Walking Eagle, the blond-haired, braided German from Emma Lee Warrior's story "Compatriots." He had walked back into history and taken a chunk of Plains Indian tradition for his own, living in a teepee resplendent with Indian art and sacred paraphernalia. I also knew that jokes ran among some Plains people about the popularity of teepees and sweat lodges and drumming circles in Germany. But here was Akiko, a woman I respected immediately, on a search parallel to mine. What had been so easy to laugh at before, the New Agers who played with religions like Birkenstock styles, swerved head-on into my own doubt about my right to take part in a culture that wasn't mine. I had the feeling that I had met the collective unconscious here in a swampy field surrounding Irish ruins. What Jung called "modern man in search of a soul" was Akiko and me.

Searches like ours have been responsible for stirring a spicy mix of Celtic symbols, runes, feathers, power-stones, and talking sticks into an appealing stew of nature reverence and navel-gazing. It seems that the flood of interest in holistic and earth-centred religions springs from some gaping chasm that yawns dangerously through the lives of Judeo-Christians. But I wondered about Akiko and me and her David, sincere as we saw ourselves. What business did we have, now that we'd lost the meaning in our own ceremonies, to appropriate bits from other cultures? And would it even work?

"I wonder why the sweat lodge is so popular in Europe," I said to Akiko.

"People are looking for something," she said. "Do you think so?"

"Yes, I do think so."

We had both come to Cahirciveen to use it as a launching place for the visit to Skellig Michael. We had both been putting it off.

"There's got to be something there," Akiko said. "Six centuries of monks. We must be able to feel something on that island."

That's what I was thinking. We were on a quest, though we couldn't name the object of our search exactly. Something. Something we had once had, or our ancestors had had, in Canada, in Ireland, in Japan. Something we had lost and knew it.

The day planned for our trip was another perfect beach day. Jeff tried to talk Akiko and me out of Skellig Michael and into the beach instead. The temptation to collapse into the hot lull of white sand and the bright holiday ease of the present was strong, a siren song luring us to forget our quest and stay, "eating the Lotos day by day, [and watching] the crisping ripples on the beach." But we had already arranged for a fisherman named Patrick to pick us up at the hostel door. On our way to the harbour, Patrick had to make several stops. He was trying to find someone to turn peat for him, a job that has to be done to ensure a good supply of dry peat bricks for heating fuel. But it was clear that at twenty pounds a head, ferrying tourists to

Skellig Michael was too lucrative an opportunity to pass up. Everyone wants to go there, it seems, except Jeff.

Skellig Michael is a pyramid of jagged black rock that juts 650 feet out of the foaming ocean seven miles off the southwest coast of Ireland. Scruffy bits of vegetation and some tenacious wildflowers cling to the craggy rock. On a calm, sunny day, like the day we approached it, the rock (you can't really call it an island) rears suddenly up out of the ocean like a threat, forbidding and dangerous, the kind of place they might exile criminals to. In stormy weather, wind and breakers slam into the rock, sweeping away anything that can't keep its clutch on the slippery stone; sea spume fizzes right over the peak. But more than one thousand years ago, a few ascetic Christian monks decided that this would be a good place to found a monastery.

They were looking for a landscape that would sculpt them into diamond-hard Christians, like the hermit monks who crawled into caves in the North African desert, fasted, and scrubbed themselves of bodily desires till they were smooth, clean shells ready to be filled by God. The Irish monks who sailed into the Atlantic looking for an environment that would test them as much as the desert must have felt a thrill of challenge when Skellig Michael cast its pointed shadow over them. Here was an impossible place, inhabited only by puffins and gannets, which took shelter in the tiny caves made when chunks of rock overlapped. No trees grew here; no animals, except the occasional seal, could be hunted for meat. The only

building material was rock. The monks would build a
monument to God, far from the comfort of other men's
routines and the clutter of soft opinion. They would start
with nothing at all.

They scrambled up to the saddle of rock five hundred
feet above sea level, turned their faces to the battering salt
wind, and exalted in the adventure this place would offer
their faith. They named the island after Michael, the
archangel of high places. God confirmed their choice with
a miracle: the lonely crag, surrounded only by ocean, held
fresh water, cradled in small pockets of rock. (Rational
minds, bothered by miracles, figured out that the fresh
water is actually rainwater, filtered down through the
rock.)

Today, the pilgrims who visit Skellig Michael are
tourists like Akiko and me. Patrick loaded fifteen of us,
mostly Germans, onto his boat in Portmagee, and we
made the gentle trip out into the ocean, with the jutting
peaks of the islands looming not far off. We didn't know
that we were lucky to have picked this super-calm day.
Though the trip is short, the swell of waves on an unsettled day can make the journey a white-knuckler, or too
dangerous altogether. Already the sun had chased the
hatless into the small shade of the boat's canvas awning.
They fiddled with cameras and squinted out at the
looming triangle islands slicing up the horizon.

We first approached Little Skellig. Patrick cut the
engine, and we heard a weird, unearthly din—anguished
cries, warning shrieks that made my mind go blank. We

glided beneath the shadow to have a look. The rock was painted white with birdshit and birds, teetering on ledges and lifting their wings menacingly. The acid stench was overpowering. There was something absolutely desolate and foreign about the scene. No human could ever live here. I was glad when the motor started up again and we got back out into the sun.

Skellig Michael has been tamed to accommodate tourists, with a dock and a concrete ramp, protected by chain-link fence, that leads to the beginning of the path up the rock face. But there were no chip stands or drinking fountains here, only lots of tourists trying to escape the unexpectedly relentless sun in all manner of makeshift hats: newspaper cones, T-shirt turbans, maps. Still, the easy landing and the anthill line of pilgrims and sightseers winding up the rock face took some of the spiritual sting out of the place.

Our group had a long climb ahead to reach the cluster of stone huts, sunk into the swoop of rock between peaks, that made up the tiny monastic settlement. The path climbed steeply and was made dangerous by loose, jagged rock. We picked our way carefully; sweat sprang up and soaked my shirt. The sun was almost directly overhead now. More men took off their shirts and wrapped them around their heads and necks. Jokes and complaints buzzed up and down the line of climbers. The smokers had to stop for a rest.

Looking down was dizzying, and I thought of the German woman I'd heard about in Clare who'd lost her life here. She was climbing this rock on a rain-slick day, her legs probably unsteady in the driving wind. She had gone off the path, Denise had told me, when everyone knew it was reckless to leave the trodden rock. Maybe she'd been trying to get away from the chatter of other tourists; maybe she'd been trying to hear the spirit of the place, off alone, perilously close to the edge. Denise said she watched her drop over the side. A Swiss woman had scrambled down after her and given her heart massage, but it was too late.

Near the top, Akiko and I crouched in the skinny shade of a rock outcrop to wait for the bottleneck of people to clear. Akiko kept us entertained by sweetly telling winded, heart-attack-red Germans, "You're halfway there!" Below us, a strange-shaped slab of rock about nine feet high seemed to face out to the sea, looking like an armless stone goddess with wide curved hips. An elderly couple in golf hats and shorts sunned themselves beside it.

At the top, the site swarmed with Americans, Italians, Germans. Two overheated student guides tried hard not to lose their patience, shooing people and their lunches off the ancient stone structures. The stone beehive cells and small oratories were built from pieces of rock found on the island and fitted together so tightly using dry stone construction (no mortar) that they remain impervious to water even today. On the hottest day in seven years, I had a hard time fixing on an image of the twelve monks tapping their tools on stone in the raw wind and bursts of cold rain, painstakingly trying to shape a rock the perfect size for the next hole. The shelters made of this sharp rock are so perfect and smooth and symmetrical, they seemed to me to be something built by insects, ants, or bees—by something genetically programmed to knit the raw materials of its environment into a viable community.

The interior of the largest cell is about thirteen by sixteen feet. I had to crouch to enter through the small doorway, which could have either acted as a constant reminder of humility or could have just been a practical way to let in less wind and rain. Standing alone in one cell, I looked up and saw a small opening in the roof. I sat in there for a couple of minutes in the semi-darkness, trying to picture the monks who had squeezed their lives into the limits of this scoop of rock. Somehow, they made a terraced vegetable garden. They buried their dead here, under the thin soil and stones, and erected rough stone crucifixes over the graves, perching their humble little cemetery on ground that overlooks the expanse of sea blending into sky. The arched window in the chapel frames a view of the mysterious Little Skellig.

In spite of their commitment to pare down their lives to spirit alone, picked clean of sensual pleasure, the place they chose hummed with a terrible beauty and they couldn't help themselves. As the small group of monks worked day after day, scrambling up and down the rock face, heaving stone into place, shaping the skellig with their bare hands, they would have had to fight back rising vanity, one of the eight capital sins laid out in the rules for monks in the Penitential of Cummean: "One who boasts of his own good deeds shall humble himself; otherwise any good he has done he has lost on account of human glory." Harder still would have been the hyper-awareness of their bodies, which ached with the burning fire of stretched, hard muscle. Alone with the smooth, curved muscle of their shoulders, their taut stomachs, the beauty of their sinewy forearms as the tight muscle turned and stretched beneath skin, they had thirty-three variations on fornication and thoughts of fornication to resist. For sodomy, seven years penance would be exacted. The mere desire to commit fornication, without the means to carry it out, carried a one-year penance. If a monk was "polluted by the violent assault of a thought" of fornication, he had to do seven days of penance. Even in sleep, he had to be vigilant. If he was "willingly polluted during sleep," or even "unintentionally polluted," he had to sing Psalms, on his knees, and fast on bread and water. But the land that could kindle their passion and vanity could also be the means of their punishment: lashings of winter wind, razors of cold rain, slices of sharp rock to mortify the flesh.

Like their pagan relatives, who found the sacred in places like springs, lakes, and oak woods, the Christian Celts intertwined their faith with place, like organisms clinging to the rock, suffering the environment, and adapting. The land became a part of their spirituality; it helped them to express it. Somewhere in making the move to Christianity, my ancestors gradually left behind this spiritual connection to places. There were no Catholic holy wells on the Niagara Peninsula, no pilgrimages to rocky places. The priests and the government were busy erasing the animism from indigenous religions, and they certainly weren't going to encourage it in the settlers. It was this connection that I, and maybe Akiko and some of the other tourists, had lost. And we were reminded of it here, in this painstaking monument to wonder and to mystery.

A ghost of that mystery brushed against me briefly in the cool, cave-like cell. Then human voices chased it away as other tourists appeared in the square of sunlight in the doorway. When I peered into the other structures, I saw other people standing quietly, listening for something just out of hearing.

On Skellig Michael, a place pared down to unadorned holiness, I thought of things that seemed holy to me: the pure desire of the monks, who had walked away from the safety of the world; the sudden splash of my healthy body cracking the still surface of a northern lake; a mother absorbed in scrubbing jam off her baby's cheeks. I wondered if I was too far gone altogether.

Last time I'd been to Mass, on Lough Derg, I had been bothered by the dryness of the church—the dry pages of the Book of Worship; the hard wooden pews; the thin, papery voices warbling uncertainly through an uninspiring hymn. The words of the prayers seemed lacking in any sense of vibrancy or gratitude. The Church had gone through a lot of changes over the years I'd been part of it. There was the move from Latin to English. Then the priest turned around to face the congregation instead of keeping his back to them. In the sixties, I had a catechism that had a hip-talking Jesus who said things to the disciples like "What are you getting so uptight about? It's just me, man." But all those changes had really made such a small difference. I read somewhere that Christians are stuck on the idea that all the major revelations have happened already; they're written in stone. We're left like children who have inherited their parents' house but aren't allowed to take any of the plastic off the lampshades, let alone buy new ones.

But Skellig Michael seemed to hold out some kind of hope. On the rock that day, I dreamed that like the Celtic monks, I could weave my religion into the place I lived. I could be touched by something truly holy thundering through my everyday life. I dreamed that like the monks, I could find a pure, rock-hard core.

On the boat ride back to Portmagee, our group was subdued. We had collectively snapped several rolls of film. We had considered the impossibility of the place, marvelled at the thousand-year-old primitive yet ingenious architecture. We had had our lunches in the sun, looking back across the heat-hazed Atlantic to the island of Ireland, and had nearly lost our footing on the treacherous path down, sending showers of stone to ping off the backs of other tourists' sunburned legs. Akiko and I had each pocketed a sharp black stone, hoping that we might feel the power of the place in the stone someday. We had been drawn to the rock by some common desire to learn the secret to the monks' purpose-drenched lives. But an unmistakable feeling of disappointment hung over our little boat. Was it worth the twenty pounds? Should we have gone to the beach instead? Karen Armstrong, in her book *A History of God,* says, "The famous tag *post coitum omne animal tristis est* still expresses a common experience: after an intense and eagerly anticipated moment, we often feel that we have missed something greater that remains just beyond our grasp."

NEWGRANGE

this place does not require your presence
and beneath the staring stars
you have discovered
your offerings are meaningless

— RANDY LUNDY, "DEER-SLEEP"

I HAD BEEN AWAY FROM HOME for five weeks and had only a couple of days left before my flight back to Canada. I had heard that Newgrange, just north of Dublin, was a passage grave about five thousand years old, older than the Egyptian pyramids. If I was going backwards in time to the spiritual landscape of this place, Newgrange was as far as I could get. Here was a place that had been dug out of the earth thousands of years ago. No one knew exactly who had built it or what it was for.

But over the centuries, the mound of earth and stone, which lined up perfectly to catch the first light of the winter solstice, continued to draw people to its secrets. Even today, it is the most visited tourist site in all of Ireland. I thought that maybe here I would find a connection to the land that went back so far, it spanned geography and culture. But when I first arrived at the site, I felt disappointed.

A few years earlier, I had been to Palenque, the Mayan ruins in Mexico, and it had been the highlight of my trip. The strange, mist-enshrouded temples, used between the seventh and ninth centuries A.D., seemed chiselled from the land itself, barely holding their ambitious human design against the hot, wet crush of jungle. Indigenous and foreign tourists laboriously climbed the steps of the Temple of Inscriptions as howler monkeys wailed and swung from the surrounding trees and the place held tight to its mysteries. One of these mysteries is that the sun's path on the day of the winter solstice is aligned with the Temple of the Inscriptions at Palenque.

Newgrange held a similar mystery. But at first glance, it seemed scrubbed clean of mystery: a sprawling expanse of uniformly shaved grass surrounded the site like a solid green towel. Except for that grass, the site seemed devoid of vegetation: not a flower, not a vine, not a tree root strayed near the neat walking paths that intersected the grounds. The mound is on high ground on the north banks of the Boyne River, with a clear view of soft green hills and a smaller unexcavated mound in the meadow to

the east. Twelve stones remain standing in what would
have been a circle around the mound. Once the area
would have been lush forest, but that all disappeared
centuries ago.

The neatness of the reconstruction of the Newgrange
tumulus startled me too. I don't know what I expected a
five-thousand-year-old structure to look like, but it wasn't
this. On the outside was a smooth rock supporting wall,
260 feet in diameter and wrapping around an even
smoother mound of earth. The wall, fronted with white
quartzite, which was discovered at the site, and studded
uniformly with round rocks the size of footballs, shim-
mered in the sunlight. It looked like a green cake in a
shiny pan, left on a counter to cool. It looked like it had
been baked half an hour ago.

But one thing stood out from the rest: lying in front of
the structure was a huge, loaf-shaped stone. It was about
ten feet long and five feet high, and it had been carved
with several spirals, some complete and others looping
into nothingness off the edges of the stone. The stone
blocked the entrance to the passage grave, a yawning
black hole framed by large slabs of putty grey rock. Above
the entrance was what looked like a smaller entrance, a
box of stone topped with a slab of rock and decorated
with a pattern of raised Xes, or what I heard described as
half-diamonds. As I looked at the spirals on the stone, Van
Gogh's *Starry Night* came immediately to mind. I had
stared at a poster of that painting during so many middles
of so many nights, working on essays in university, that I

was intimately familiar with the wild swirls of stars, the
lines of blue and black and yellow sweeping through the
sky. As I laboured with theses and paragraphs, struggling
to hammer ideas into some coherent order, *Starry Night*
was like a joyful abandonment into the beauty of the
unknowable. The spiral carvings at Newgrange had a
similar effect on me. I stood there for a long time, drawn
into the swirl of spirals that hinted at some chaotic but
comforting flow, when an order gradually forced itself
onto my consciousness: specifically, that the only people
going into the dark hole of the passageway were those
with the proper colour-coded tag.

I made my way back up the clean path to the kiosk
where tags were distributed. I had yellow. More than
seventy thousand people a year come to Newgrange.
Seventy thousand shoulders brush up against the ancient
stone carvings as they squeeze through the narrow
passageway. One hundred and forty thousand feet tread
over the mathematically aligned ground. Seven hundred
thousand fingers brush gently along the forty-three damp
upright stones lining the passageway. About eleven
million pounds of flesh shake the earth and stone founda-
tions. With that kind of traffic going through there, I was
grateful it hadn't been sealed up years ago in a mad panic
of archeological preservation and an imitation built for
tourists instead.

But I envied the workman who had rediscovered the
passage in the seventeenth century. T. W. Rolleston tells how
the men were searching for stone to use in a road-building

project when they came upon the entrance to the tomb
and realized that there was a passageway into the interior.
Did they leave their tools and crawl through the opening,
going deeper and deeper into a mystery as thick as the
darkness? Did they touch the smooth stone bowls and feel
the wonder of the place before all the theories and expla-
nations came thundering in on it?

Finally, the yellow group was called. Steps are built
around the spiral entrance stone to keep tourists off it, but
originally, you would have had to crawl over the stone to
enter the passageway. Some researchers see the spirals as
representations of fingerprints. Others think the spirals
represent the journey of the soul through life and death to
rebirth. We had to duck to enter the narrow passage built
of massive stone slabs, twenty-one on one side, twenty-
two on the other. Electric light dimly illuminated the
passage, and I could make out more spirals on the inside
walls. The passage slants gradually upwards, over the
sixty feet that lead to the inner chamber. In this circular
chamber, the twelve of us were able to stand up straight.
Nooks were recessed in three directions around the
chamber, with smooth stone bowls in each. Remnants of
burnt human bone were found in the bowls, but these
make up the remains of only about five humans. Since the
sites have been disturbed over the centuries, it is impossible to know if this was the extent of the burials there.

The guide explained that the construction of the tight
stone roof was so carefully planned that in forty-odd
centuries, no water has leaked through. Gutters carved

into the roof slabs carry away rainwater. Our group crowded around in a circle, gazing up.

One of the biggest mysteries about Newgrange was rediscovered in the 1960s by Prof. M. J. O'Kelly. He had begun excavation work on the tumulus and had heard about a local rumour that at a certain time of year, a ray of sun would light up the inside of the grave. Professor O'Kelly calculated that this could happen only in the winter, when the angle of the sun would be low enough to shine into the entrance. In the winter of 1969, he went by himself into the inner chamber of the grave and waited for the first sunrise of the winter solstice. In an interview with writer James Charles Roy, he described the experience: "I was there entirely alone, inside the tomb, looking down the passage towards the slit [the roof-box opening], gradually seeing the sky going from gray to pink, and finally the tip of the disk of the sun appeared above, over the horizon, which is a hill about three miles away, and then this shaft of light striking straight in right the length of the passage and into the centre of the tomb."

"I wonder why the orientation to the winter solstice," someone in our yellow group asked.

"Some astronomers speculate that the site could have been used for an astronomical observatory," the guide said. "But that doesn't explain the human remains."

"Couldn't the ray of light just be a coincidence?" someone else wondered.

"It's possible," the guide allowed. There were some snorts of doubt from the group.

"I wonder what the spirals out front have to do with it," another voice asked.

"Probably the construction company's logo," said an American man. General guffaws. We wanted answers. We were getting none.

The highlight of the tour was to be an electrical simulation of the phenomenon that takes place at the winter solstice. It had already occurred to me to come back on that day to experience it, but it had already occurred to thousands of others too. Visits for that date are booked years ahead, with more than a thousand names on the waiting list.

"The light will be extinguished for about a minute," the guide warned.

With the light went our chattering. The chamber fell silent and dark. I instinctively looked up, searching for a point of light. Blood thundered against my temples. The dark void swam around me. I reached out, afraid I was about to tip over. Then it came. A tiny ray of light. It grew longer till light filled the hushed chamber. I felt tears filling my eyes, and a rush of feeling caught in my throat. Then a collective breath was released, and with the light, the chatter and jokes filled the chamber again.

It was the red group's turn, so we were ushered out. I blinked in the bright sunlight as I emerged. I looked for my bearings: ticket kiosk over there, interpretive centre over there, bus loop up there. What this lump was that had lodged in my chest, I didn't know. But I thought I was going to cry and didn't want to be caught crying like a lost child in this throng of people. I crossed the road and found a tree to sit under. I took some deep breaths. Maybe I was just lonely. I'd been away from home too long.

A small wind moved through the branches of the tree above me. It wasn't a tree I recognized: deep green glossy leaves, a drooping rounded shape. Maybe a hawthorn? The sky was soft turquoise, washed out to white where it met the hill in the distance. The wind carried a faintly familiar smell. It was the kind of day when a tourist might think, I wonder if I could live here, rent a little cottage in Clare, spend my days walking the cliffs and writing by the turf fire.

I thought about our yellow group's desire to shape a coherent reason for the mystery of Newgrange. Because of the winter solstice alignment, astronomers have theorized that Newgrange could have been used as a calendar to keep watch for times of important ceremonies. Professor O'Kelly feels sure that the site involved spiritual celebration of some kind, something beyond simple burial of the dead. I talked to a woman who was sure that Newgrange was a goddess-worshipping site. What I called spirals, she called concentric circles, representing the virgin, the mother, and the crone.

My favourite Newgrange story came from an old Celtic myth that claims that the tumulus was the fairy palace of the Danaan prince Angus Og, the Irish god of love. His wife, the princess, had a beautiful servant named Ethne. One day, it was discovered that Ethne never ate. It seems that a Danaan chieftain had been visiting the palace and was overwhelmed by Ethne's beauty. He tried to take her by force, and this violence sparked a moral outrage in Ethne that was characteristic of humans and not fairies. The story goes that after that, she was nourished by God's will, instead of fairy food. But on a warm summer day, when some of the maidens were bathing in the river Boyne, Ethne discovered she had lost her fairy veil of invisibility, the veil that gave her the ability to pass between the human and fairy worlds unseen by human eyes. When she tried to find her way back to the entrance to the palace at Newgrange, she couldn't. Instead, she came upon a walled garden with a monastery inside. A monk brought Ethne to St. Patrick, who adopted her into the human family. (Ethne would have been fifteen hundred years old when she met St. Patrick.) But Ethne was praying one day when she heard a rushing in the air and the hum of fairy voices, like bees in a hive, calling her name. She was overcome with longing for her fairy life and died a short time later.

Ethne's story sounded like the story of the Irish themselves, the ancient entrances to the secret place under the earth lost to them, Christianity providing a pale substitute. It sounded like my own story. In the Newgrange chamber, I thought that I had heard the faint rushing in my ears, too, the sound of the secret world I longed for but couldn't find.

I HAD BEEN DRIVEN by the same longing in Canada. Just a few minutes north of Saskatoon is one of about one hundred medicine wheels that remain on the northern plains of North America. Its age and the mysteries it holds are almost the same as Newgrange's. For thousands of years, right up to about two hundred years ago, this was a special gathering place for Plains people. In 1982, extensive excavation began on the site, and it was named Wanuskewin, which is Cree for "seeking peace of mind."

I drove up one early spring day doing just that. I had left my Valiant at home and rented a car for the day, a brand-new Chevy Impala with cruise control. I sailed out of Regina with a Styrofoam cup of tea in the cup holder, my legs crossed comfortably, and Mozart's twelve variations on "Twinkle, Twinkle Little Star" on the radio. There's nothing like cruise control on the Prairies in a car that rides like a sailing vessel. Out the windshield, a sea of washed-out pastels—pale blue sky, straw yellow fields— dotted with licorice black crows. Paper bag brown cattails and orange reeds stood in ponds crusted with ice. The land is sliced up by hydro wires and fences, but if I closed my eyes just enough to blur my vision (keeping a couple of fingers on the wheel to navigate), the wires disappeared and I pictured a time before the coming of the "steel rope," which Cree people had prophesied.

When I arrived at the Wanuskewin site, I opened the car door and the wind ripped it from my grasp. It was the last week of March, sunny and above zero after a week of bitter cold, but the wind made me glad I'd brought my hat and mitts. After a brief stop inside the interpretive centre, I took the trail that led to the medicine wheel. The medicine wheel is contained within a three-hundred-acre archeological site on a wide prairie rich in resources like the buffalo. Archeologists have known about this area since the 1930s. Elders from the nearby Beardy Okemasis reserve remembered stories about the gathering place that existed in the Opimihaw Creek valley, near the South Saskatchewan River. The trail dropped quickly into the creek valley, out of the worst of the wind. But the noise of the wind was incessant, hissing through the dry grass around me and roaring like a waterfall across the cliffs up above me that were once used as buffalo jumps. As I walked, I could see why the place was named the way it was; I could feel tension I didn't know I had sliding off my shoulders like ice thaws dropping off the riverbank.

Footprints marked the path, human, deer, and coyote criss-crossing over each other in the mud. Everything else seemed bone-dry. Bare poplar, aspen, and cottonwood creaked and clicked their skeleton branches against each other. Pale orange grass rustled stiffly in the wind. Rust-coloured lichen crusted over rocks. Wild rose bushes and low junipers held on to a few dried-up berries. I was alone on the trail, but in the tumult of the wind, I thought I heard voices. I kept thinking that around the curve of the path I would run into a crowd of other tourists, but I didn't pass one other person along the trail. As I came nearer to the bank of the South Saskatchewan River, I could see geese steadying themselves in the wind, coming in for a landing on the open water. Their raucous honks carried on the wind like children calling to each other.

Excavation has revealed at least thirteen different layers of occupation for Wanuskewin, going back six thousand years. Obsidian from the Rocky Mountains has been found, along with pottery from Missouri and other trade goods from across North America. But as at Newgrange, the artifacts didn't tell the whole story. In among the trees beside the path, I caught sight of pieces of coloured cloth—red, green, blue, white, yellow—tied around tree trunks in some places. They whipped stiffly in the wind, their colours fading. Though the official tourist plaques seemed cautiously understated about the spiritual nature of this place, the cloth was a reminder that people still live close to the mysteries that these rocks and trees hold.

The trail curved up out of the wooded coulee to a sweep of rock-studded meadow. I climbed the path to a ledge of ground higher than everything around it. The wind hammered me fiercely up there, so that I had to tuck my chin into my shoulders to catch my breath. I looked for something to protect me from the wind's battering. There was only the concrete viewing platform that had been built to look out over the medicine wheel. I hunkered down in the V between the land and the concrete. From my sheltered spot, I couldn't see a lot of the medicine wheel, just a faint circle worn in the grass and an overgrown cairn of rocks in what I assumed was the middle of the wheel. A wire-and-post fence surrounded the wheel.

At one end of the fenced area were what looked like small teepee rings. Earlier, I had wondered what teepee rings were for. The modern-day canvas teepees I'd seen in

British Columbia held their own without the support of rocks. But now I understood clearly. I could imagine the wild flapping of hides and the pole frames shuddering and bending in the relentless wind.

What I wondered next was why this spot, which caught the worst pummelling of the wind, would be chosen for anything. But as I stood and braved the wind to get a better look, the spectacular view hit me full on: the soft curves of the hills; the dark dips into secret woods; the broad snake of the river; the grass plains beyond, softly shadowed like a face. But the view of the sky stretched even farther, a blue three times bigger than the land, extending right off the edges of vision. The sun was almost directly overhead at this time of day. Had it been night, the view of the stars would have been as unobstructed as it could be in any place on earth.

Various theories exist about the purpose of the plains medicine wheels. John A. Eddy, an astronomer, has studied medicine wheels across the U.S. and Canadian plains. All of them have clear views of the sky in all directions. He found that the Bighorn medicine wheel in Wyoming, which has twenty-eight stone spokes radiating from the centre, and the Moose Mountain wheel in southern Saskatchewan, with five radiating spokes, both have their central rock cairns aligned to the first light of the summer solstice. He also found correlations with other cairns and the bright stars of Aldebaran, Rigel, and Sirius. He believes that the wheels might have acted as calendars, to signal the start of the solstice, as well as the time for ceremonies. Some archeologists think that the medicine wheels that don't show an obvious alignment with the sun or the stars could be more recent constructions, built as monuments to important people. Other theories suggest they were used as burial grounds.

Mark Wolfleg Sr., a Blackfoot elder who was interviewed in 1983, said he didn't know what the wheels in Alberta were for. "The wheels are ancient," he said. Joe Duquette, a Cree elder who was asked about the medicine wheels, also in 1983, said, "Before they used to go there and pick the stones because they were holy or something like that, precious, you know. They used to do their ceremonies in the summer time and pray there, you know. . . . They loved this medicine wheel. Otherwise, after that I don't know what they do, you know, but that is what I was told." Many Cree elders in Saskatchewan agree that these wheels were built before the time of the Cree. In fact, there is no word in Cree for "medicine wheel." The term apparently came from Europeans, who saw a resemblance to wagon wheels in the pattern of rocks on the ground. The word "medicine" suggests the power of the ceremonies presumed to have taken place there.

Medicine-wheel ceremonies go on today, though few people claim it is an unbroken tradition, unchanged from ancient times. Versions of the ceremony vary across North America, but most seem to use the wheel as a symbol of the human journey. Some, like the one we attended in British Columbia, have the participants plant a rock from their area in the wheel. Some connect different directions with human attributes. When I was reading about Yeats's spiral, I was surprised to come across his wheel theory: a circle intersected by twenty-eight spokes, with the four human faculties, the will, the creative mind, the body of fate, and the mask, slicing the wheel into quarters. I wondered what he'd been reading. Or was the wheel symbol so old and so ubiquitous that Yeats was tapping into the collective unconscious, like his wife with her automatic writing, scribbling down notes from the other side?

Crouching by the fence, I looked through the squares of wire. A curve of sun-bleached bone lay inside the circle. Probably like most other visitors, I wondered what would happen if I could sit inside the fenced area, if some cosmic order would be magically revealed to me. I noticed that a path was worn from around the last fencepost right up to the central cairn. Was this part of the original configuration, or had it been made by countless visitors' feet, sneaking around the barrier when no one was looking? Too conscious of being an outsider, I wasn't willing to test it myself.

The path offered me another theory about this medicine wheel at Wanuskewin. Maybe the circle could have been formed not by a collection of rocks, like at some other sites around the prairies, but by a circle of feet. If the area was considered sacred ground, it seems logical that not everyone would have camped inside the wheel. The wind on the high open prairie would have kept the area free from mosquitoes, as the tourist plaque says. But it would also have made for uncomfortable camping—flicking cooking fires dangerously in all directions, whipping hair into faces, picking up loose objects and flinging them into the sky. The scalp-searing summer sun would have been inescapable too. It is more likely that most people who gathered for the ceremonies would have chosen camping areas in the calmer coulees, maybe near the cooling water of the creek. I think the wheel itself must have been a gathering place for spiritual celebration. For the fifteen hundred or so years that archeologists think this wheel has existed here, people might have stood together on this high ground to celebrate the beauty they could see stretched out in all directions around them. Even on a bland spring day, as I peered through the wire of a fence, I felt giddy with fullness, a spark of something huge and mysterious crackling through my veins.

I had been told that at a place like this I should leave something as an offering for what I am taking away. I opened a pouch of tobacco I had bought for the purpose in Saskatoon. The wind snatched a pinch of it from between my fingers and carried it through the fence, where the dry grass caught it in the cairn of the medicine wheel.

Back in the shelter of my rental car, I turned the heat up and pressed the button to automatically adjust the back-rest. My hair had been whipped to the consistency of a broom and my hands were stiff with cold. As I drove back out onto the highway, the smell of fresh Drum tobacco filled the car. Somewhere south of Saskatoon, I pulled off on a side road leading nowhere and rolled myself a smoke. I found myself in the paradoxical position of being both drawn to the mystery of the medicine wheel and driven to understand what it was for. Uncertainty hounded me.

As I drew on my smoke in the plush comfort of the Impala, I was tempted to do what the scholar and writer Sam D. Gill cautions against: see the circle of the wheel as a simple representation of harmony and balance and equality. My own idealized image was a hot summer night in July, the laughter of children playing, the smell of meat roasting over the fire, spiritually enlightened adults gazing up at the stars, reflecting on the blessings of the past year. But Gill explains, "This image of the 'Indian' sacred circle tends to amplify a highly romantic picture of peoples living in harmony and peace with each other and nature. It is not a realistic view of human life for peoples whose entire histories have been filled with hardship, disease, death, discomfort and difficulties." His caution was another reminder that I was far from understanding the complexity of this intimate relationship with the land.

But there is an undeniable resonance to the spirals and stone dome of Newgrange and the stones of the medicine wheel, and this resonance draws people from the four corners of the world. For Jung, the mandala, or wheel, was a collective symbol of the wholeness of the psyche: thought, feeling, intuition, and sensation. Even the Christian cross is a form of the mandala. At one time, the equilateral cross was the symbol Christians used, a balance of fours that suggested the circle. But over time, the centre edged upwards, reflecting the Christian exaltation of the spirit above the earth and the body. The earth and the body became prisons to escape from. This psychic imbalance is what the wheel symbolism unconsciously seeks to repair.

I finished my smoke and was tempted to dump the whole contents of the tobacco pouch onto the prairie to keep the sweet smell from tempting me to roll another. Jung says that collective symbols cannot be thought up; they grow naturally from the "forgotten depths" to express "what thought cannot think." The crossbeam on the twenty-first-century cross was mounted so firmly in the realm of intellect, it was hard to admit something that could not be thought through. But there they were, the tumulus of Newgrange and the medicine wheel at Wanuskewin, stirring some forgotten memory, unknowable and irresistible, like perfect round stones on the beach that I had to pick up and hold in my hand.

I LEFT NEWGRANGE still rattled and caught a bus to Dublin, where I found a bed at a nice modern hostel in a central part of town. When I went to locate my bed, I found the room already occupied by two heavily cologne-scented men who I thought were speaking Spanish, but turned out to be speaking English—they were from Scotland. Sharing a room with strangers was bad enough, but sharing with men really overstepped my comfort boundaries. To make matters worse, they were friendly. I was as rude as my Canadian sensibility would allow, but they took it as teasing and tried to share their vodka and joints, insisting I have fun with them with the good-hearted aggressiveness of Ukrainian grandmothers forcing me to eat more perogies. I decided to try the same tactic I had used in Doolin: I went to the main desk and begged for a private room.

"What's the problem?" the desk clerk asked.

"It's just that my roommates are already drinking, and I have the feeling I won't get a very good sleep," I said.

Just then, one of the Scottish men emerged from the stairs into the lobby.

"Hey! Are you drinking up there?" the desk clerk shouted at him. The Scot looked straight at me.

"No, no!" he said cheerfully in his Scottish accent.

"You'd better not be, because there's no drinking allowed in the rooms," warned the clerk.

"Right!" the Scot said, waving to me on his way out.

"I didn't know drinking wasn't allowed in the rooms," I said sheepishly.

"We're right full," the clerk said. "If they bother you, just let me know."

Great. He'd really solved that problem for me. Now I had to share a room with two big Scots, well into their vodka and pot, who thought I was a spoilsport and a snitch. I left the hostel and walked. I stopped on a bridge over the river Liffey. It was evening, still daylight, but the light was soft and pinkish, coloured by the orange-red brick buildings crowding the narrow streets. I had been

reading *A Portrait of the Artist As a Young Man,* and
Stephen Dedalus's little-boy reflection came to me: "But
you could not have a green rose. But perhaps somewhere
in the world you could." I crossed the bridge and saw a
phone booth and slipped inside to call David in Canada.
When I heard his voice on the other end, I burst into tears.

THE CLOSER I CAME to leaving Ireland, the more I felt
I'd already crossed back over the ocean in my heart. This
wasn't my home. If I tried to live here, I'd be perpetually
homesick. But what home was I returning to? Ontario
could never be my home either. There was nothing there
that really belonged to me any more. Long ago, my ancestors began to be alienated from a homeland. What began
when the British alienated so many Irish from their land
over here continued even today.

My ancestor Nicholas Smith was among the first white
settlers on the Niagara Peninsula after the American
Revolution. He settled on land that had been surrendered
by the Mississauga in 1784 with Colonel Butler's encouragement, a huge area also covering the Grand River valley
and the north shore of Lake Erie, in total more than two
and a half million acres. The land was not surrendered by
treaty but "purchased" by the British in exchange for
£1,100 of trade goods.

The Iroquois were Nicholas's friends, fellow Loyalists
he fought alongside during the war. In 1785, the same
year that Nicholas received his Crown grant in Lincoln
County, the Mohawk leader Thayendanegea, or Joseph

Brant, led two thousand Iroquois Loyalists north to the
Grand River valley in Upper Canada. The Mohawks
chose the area centring around present-day Brantford for
their home, while other Iroquois spread along the river
stretching down to Lake Erie, an area covering about six
hundred thousand acres. While the Iroquois understood
this to be an agreement that the land was their own, not
unlike the Crown grants the white Loyalists had received,
the British acted like overprotective parents, maintaining
the final word on any decisions about the land. The
Iroquois' land base was gradually eaten away, so that
the present Six Nations reserve is a fraction of the land
originally promised.

What for my ancestors was a fresh start, full of opportunity, became for the Iroquois a sad and unsatisfactory
compromise. They were confined to a region now stripped
of its wildlife and expected to rely only on farming, a job
that Iroquois men considered "women's work." When
Nicholas walked from the Niagara Peninsula to see how
his fellow soldiers, the Mohawks, were getting along, I
wonder if he perceived the chasm that every day seemed
to be widening between them.

Half a century later, when the Dillons and Leonards
arrived from Ireland, they settled on the other side of Lake
Ontario, around Cobourg. By that time, the Ojibwa, or
Anishinabe, people had been pushed away from the land
around Lake Ontario to the lakes farther north. Cobourg
in the middle of the nineteenth century was, according to
Susanna Moodie, a "thriving, populous town, and it has

trebled its population during the lapse of twenty years."
Her sister, Catharine Parr Traill, in her *Canadian Settler's
Guide,* enthuses, "It is a pleasant thing to contemplate the
growing prosperity of a new country. To see thriving
farmers, with well-stored barns, and sunny pastures
covered with flocks and herds; with fruitful gardens and
orchards, extending over spaces where once lay the track-
less and impenetrable forest; and to reflect that these
things have been the result of industry and well-directed
energy." But as the settlers flourished, the indigenous
experience played an ominous counter-theme of alienation, from both their land and their way of life. The
settlers neglected to acknowledge the depth of the intimate relationship that the indigenous people had with the
land. To acknowledge it, they would have had to admit to
playing a role too despicable to contemplate. But when
they ignored that relationship, they began the process of
ignoring their own.

NIGHT-TIME IN DUBLIN. Quiet room. The Scottish
men had gone out and I was calm again after talking to
David. Warm orange streetlight streamed in next to my
bed near the window, softening the darkness in the room.
The rattle of diesel engines and tinny horns echoed off the
walls in the narrow street. A sooty, diesel smell wafted
through the window on the warm breeze like a Dublin
cologne.

I wasn't really trying to sleep, though I was lying in bed
in the dark; it's just that there was no bedside lamp in the

room. I considered trying to read *A Portrait of the Artist As a Young Man* by the Dublin streetlight, but that would have meant climbing down from my bunk to get the book out of my pack, and I could already feel my limbs sinking comfortably into the mattress. I thought about Newgrange and the medicine wheels. Looking to the familiar patterns of stars could be a migratory people's answer to carrying a place with them. It could work for a migrant like me. On the edge of sleep, I felt the dizzying moment of darkness in the Newgrange chamber sweep over me. For a few seconds, I held on to the feeling, something familiar: grief, comfort, confusion, gratitude. It was the same puzzling rush of emotions that had swept over me in the sweat lodge. I was in Ireland, at the end of a pilgrimage I'd made with my mother's voice constantly close to my ear. I had made the pilgrimage she should have made. Her carefully written notes in the turquoise ink had led me finally back to the beginning, to the womb of earth, where we all began.

HOME

*I need wolf's eyes to see
the truth.*

—MARGARET ATWOOD, "FURTHER ARRIVALS"

I FLEW BACK TO TORONTO with ten Irish pounds in my pocket. At the airport, waiting for my connection to Regina, I converted the pounds to Canadian dollars and went to the cafeteria for a cup of tea and a plate of french fries and gravy. A handsome cashier with his sturdy jaw nicked from shaving handed me my change and said, "You have a good day, eh?" His twangy little accent filled me with a ridiculous sense of well-being. I was home.

On the plane, as I looked out over the wing, even the sky seemed familiar: a blue like a favourite blanket, white cumulus clouds puffed like popcorn and tearing apart now and then to give me a glimpse of green squares of prairie below. When I had left, the fields were still a dull palette of greyed browns and yellows from winter, but now, in July, they were a brief, vivid green.

When Anne and Rose, Hugh Dillon and Hugh Smith, Mary Bethel and Mary Miskella came to this country, this landscape was a foreign place of maple trees eighteen feet in diameter and pine forests so thick no light penetrated the gloom below. Frances Stewart, a fellow Irishwoman from County Antrim, lamented in a letter to a friend: "I often think of the happiness it would be to return home, than to live as we do here in a never-ending scene of bustle, turmoil and hard work. Now but three years are over, [and] though we have a fine light wide opening in the woods and ten acres of promising wheat under the snow . . . yet there is a degree of anxiety and wearying hurry for ever which prevents inside comfort." But she added, "If we live long enough this will be a lovely place."

One hundred and fifty years later, it is not only the place that has changed: the place has changed us. The smells of pine and cedar, the sound of rising and falling coyote songs, the colour of the sunlight on a cold fall day, became part of our collective memories, passed on in the blood through each generation.

I could see the sudden fuzz of houses and cluster of shining office towers of Regina, rising up out of an expanse of fields. Regina holds the dubious distinction of having planted all its trees by hand. It still has that "barely under our control" feeling: a neat, deliberate little city expanding outwards in improbably tidy squares on a wind-whipped, flat, dry prairie softened only by the dribble of a creek edged with willow. But I'd only been living here a few months. I knew that this place too would work on me little by little.

THE ONLY THING I SAW when I got off the plane was David, tall and calm and smiling, leaning against a pillar, his skin tanned and his soft hair black against his white T-shirt. When I hugged him, he smelled like summer, the light fresh-breeze smell of cotton and the deep warm-sun smell of skin.

On the drive home from the airport, I saw the city had been transformed from the spindly barrenness of spring to a lush, green, and grown-over burst of fertility. Morden red roses and hot pink peonies were crushed against picket fences. Farms had sprung up in backyards—neat rows of peas, pole beans, lettuce, potatoes, tomatoes. Our own backyard seemed exotic, with its large, craggy crabapple tree spreading shade over half the yard and our two cats laying low in the grass, sniffing the loaded air. David had planted a little garden of tomatoes, squash, lettuce, radishes, and basil. The radishes were already big enough to eat.

Everything about home was wonderful: a hot bath in our deep, old clawfoot bathtub, surrounded by bottles of shampoo, bars of soap and candles, clean towels on the shelf, and a cold glass of homemade lemonade. I washed out my travel clothes and a few of David's clothes and hung them on the line; the sun was touching the fabric and drying it as I watched the line of damp shrinking. And David, so capable and steady, who had gone out on his bike to get some cream for our afternoon coffee.

In the evening, yellow clouds thickened in the east and thunder rumbled in the distance, building, rolling closer. We could smell the rain, but only a few drops spattered on the cracked concrete of the patio as we sat there waiting. The storm didn't come, just the low rumbles and the scent of it, making the ripe smell of fresh-cut grass and cottonwood trees even richer. It wasn't until 3 a.m. that a thundercrack loud enough to shake the house ripped overhead, splitting the clouds open like some mad cook with a machete.

David and I sat up in bed, he with a big grin on his face in the white lightning flash. He threw open the back door (which in our strange little rental house was in our bedroom) in what had become almost a nightly ritual for him while I was away. Growing up on the West Coast, David had never experienced the ferocity of a Prairie summer storm. The first time he'd stood outside on the patio watching in amazement, the detonation of one thunderbolt so close it popped a transformer at the end of the lane made him drop to his knees on the concrete.

We stood under the eaves of the house and watched the lightning spider above the trees and light up the whole sky with explosive cracks. Then the rain came, big drops splatting the leaves of the crabapple, the clothes left on the line, the patio, the still-warm vinyl siding of the house, the screen windows, and us. The splats came faster and harder till they merged into one rushing, furious downpour. Usually the storm spends itself with the rain, but this one was just getting started. A few more thundercracks let loose the wind. The branches of the tall cottonwoods in our neighbours' yards pitched in wild figure eights. The poplars bent almost to the ground. David ran outside under the pretense of rescuing the kitchen chairs we'd left under the crabapple tree, but it was really just to feel the thrill of danger that had descended on this predictable Prairie town. As he grabbed the chairs, the wind snapped a large branch of the crabapple tree and left it hanging precariously, and someone's blue tarp came flapping across the lane like a huge bat, plastering itself against our fence.

"Get inside!" I shouted. I was sure a tornado was bearing down on us, and us with no basement to hide in, just these four flimsy vinyl-and-wood walls. As he brought in the rescued chairs, the wind ripped the door out of his hand and slammed it against the house with such force I thought the hinges would give way.

David was soaking wet but exhilarated. I dried him off and we watched the storm through the back door, waiting for our insubstantial house to get airborne and sail out over the more solid houses of our neighbourhood.

The next morning I slept late. I woke up to the smell of a humid breeze and a curtain billowing gently at the window. The thick summer heat held me suspended in a haze of pure memory: the hot, damp after-storm smell; the sound of excited birds in the tree by the window. A door slammed by itself in the quiet, empty house. For a moment I was back at our house on Pelham Road, in the room I shared with my little brother. During afternoon naps, when the breeze swept through the window screens in the quiet house, I studied the things my mother had hung on our pale blue walls: a picture of a haloed, golden-haired girl, her chubby hands clutched in prayer; a creamy white crucifix holding a golden Jesus, and behind it, a bunch of dried palm leaves.

My Irish ancestors carried within them a certainty about who they were and the Catholic faith that defined them. That certainty eludes me. But my mother had tended this faith as carefully as she did her precious roses on the farm on Pelham Road. I still had the crucifix in a box somewhere in storage. I was seized with a sudden desire to retrieve it, not to let this connection disappear completely.

The phone rang, the first call from my sisters welcoming me home, wondering what I had found out. Outside I could see David cleaning up debris from the storm in the steaming July heat. Propped against my open backpack near the phone was a bodhran I had brought home, painted with interlocking Celtic designs in green and gold. I had brought back my own Celtic knot of conjecture, truth, and desires, criss-crossing over each other in a continuous loop. Where to begin?

SOURCES

CHAPTER ONE

A Catechism of Christian Doctrine. Baltimore: Confraternity of Christian Doctrine, 1941.

Catechism of the Catholic Church. New York: Image Doubleday, 1995.

Joyce, Alice. *Oral History Film Project Collection*. Regina: Canadian Plains Research Centre.

Kane, Margo. "Moonlodge." In *An Anthology of Canadian Native Literature in English,* edited by David Daniel Moses and Terry Goldie. Toronto: Oxford University Press, 1992.

McCarthy, Tony. *The Irish Roots Guide*. Dublin: The Lilliput Press, 1991.

Ruffo, Armand Garnet. "She Asked Me." In *Geronimo's Grave*. Regina: Coteau Books, 2001.

CHAPTER TWO

Birney, Earle. "Bushed." In *The Collected Poems of Earle Birney*, 2 vols. Toronto: McClelland & Stewart, 1975.

Dittrick, Capt. James. *Loyalist Narratives of Upper Canada*. Edited by James Talman. Toronto: The Champlain Society, 1946.

Greeley, Susan Burnham. *Loyalist Narratives of Upper Canada*. Edited by James Talman. Toronto: The Champlain Society, 1946.

Harris, Amelia. *Loyalist Narratives of Upper Canada*. Edited by James Talman. Toronto: The Champlain Society, 1946.

Jung, Carl, ed. *Man and His Symbols*. New York: Dell Publishing, 1964.

Magrath, Thomas William. *Authentic Letters from Upper Canada: Including an Account of Canadian Field Sports* [*c.* 1833]. Toronto: Macmillan, 1953.

McGee, Thomas D'Arcy. *A History of the Irish Settlers in North America, from the Earliest Period to the Census of 1850*. Boston: Office of the American Celt, 1851.

Moodie, Susanna. *Roughing It in the Bush*. Toronto: McClelland and Stewart, 1989.

Traill, Catharine Parr. *The Backwoods of Canada*. Toronto: McClelland and Stewart, 1966.

Turner, Frederick W. *Beyond Geography: The Western Spirit against the Wilderness*. New York: Viking Press, 1980.

CHAPTER THREE

Cowan, Tom. *Fire in the Head: Shamanism and the Celtic Spirit*. New York: HarperSanFrancisco, 1993.

Woodham-Smith, Cecil. *The Great Hunger.* New York: Old
  Town Books, 1962.

Yeats, William Butler. *Writings on Irish Folklore, Legend and
  Myth.* London: Penguin Books, 1993.

CHAPTER FOUR

Carlson, Keith Thor, ed. *You Are Asked to Witness: The Stó:lō
  in Canada's Pacific Coast History.* Chilliwack: Stó:lō Heritage
  Trust, 1997.

Jaffé, Aniela. *Man and His Symbols.* Carl Jung, ed. New York:
  Dell Publishing, 1964.

Jones, Peter. *History of the Ojebway Indians: With Especial
  Reference to Their Conversion to Christianity.* London:
  A. W. Bennett, 1861. (Made available online by Early
  Canadiana Online: www.canadiana.org/eco.)

Lonesinger, Antoine. *Oral History Film Project Collection.*

Rolleston, T. W. *Myths and Legends of the Celtic Race.* 2d ed.
  London: George G. Harrap and Co. Ltd., 1911.

Williames, Tracie. *Oral History Film Project Collection.*

Woodham-Smith. *The Great Hunger.*

Yeats. *Writings on Irish Folklore, Legend and Myth.*

CHAPTER FIVE

Davies, Oliver, trans. *Celtic Spirituality.* New Jersey: Paulist
  Press, 1999.

De Marchi, John. *Fatima from the Beginning.* 6th ed. Fátima,
  Portugal: Missões Consolata, 1986.

CHAPTER SIX

Manuel, George, and Michael Posluns. *The Fourth World: An
  Indian Reality.* Don Mills, Ont.: Collier Macmillan Canada,
  1974.

McGee, Thomas D'Arcy. *Catholic History of North America.*
  Boston: P. Donahoe, 1855.

McLeod, Neal. "Coming Home Through Stories." *International Journal of Canadian Studies* 18 (Fall 1998): 51–66.

Miller, J. R. *Sweet Promises: A Reader on Indian–White Relations in Canada.* Toronto: University of Toronto Press, 1991.

Chapter Seven

Cowan. *Fire in the Head.*

Duffy, Joseph. *Lough Derg Guide.* Lough Derg, Ireland: St. Patrick's Purgatory, 1978.

Fox, Matthew. *Original Blessing.* Santa Fe, N. Mex.: Bear and Company, 1983.

St. Augustine. *Confessions.* London: Penguin Books, 1961.

St. Patrick. *The Works of St. Patrick.* Translated by Ludwig Bieler. Westminster, Md.: Newman Press, 1953.

Chapter Eight

Costigan, Giovanni. *A History of Modern Ireland.* New York: Pegasus, 1969.

Daily Globe, The. Toronto, July 13, 1870.

Dues, Greg. *Catholic Customs and Traditions.* Mystic, Conn.: Twenty-third Publications, 1989.

Harris, William Richard. *The Catholic Church in the Niagara Peninsula, 1626–1895.* Toronto: Briggs, 1895.

Houston, Cecil J., and William J. Smyth. *The Sash Canada Wore: A Historical Geography of the Orange Order in Canada.* Toronto: University of Toronto Press, 1980.

Irish Canadian. Toronto, March 22, 1871.

Kealey, Gregory S., and Peter Warrian, eds. *Essays in Canadian Working-Class History.* Toronto: McClelland and Stewart, 1976.

Kee, Robert. *Ireland: A History.* London: Weidenfeld and Nicolson, 1980.

Keegan, Gerald. *Famine Diary: Journey to a New World.* Dublin: Wolfhound, 1991.

Moodie, Susanna. *Life in the Clearings versus the Bush.* Toronto: McClelland and Stewart, 1989.

O'Driscoll, Robert, and Lorna Reynolds, eds. *The Untold Story: The Irish in Canada.* 2 vols. Toronto: Celtic Arts of Canada, 1988.

Senior, Hereward. *Orangeism: The Canadian Phase.* Toronto: McGraw-Hill Ryerson, 1972.

Smith, Donald B. *Sacred Feathers: The Reverend Peter Jones and the Mississauga Indians.* Toronto: University of Toronto Press, 1987.

St. Brendan. *Navigato Sancti Brendani abbatis* (The Voyage of St. Brendan: Journey to the promised land). Translated and with an introduction by John J. O'Meara. Atlantic Highlands, N.J.: Humanities Press, 1976.

Whyte, Robert. Robert *Whyte's 1847 Famine Ship Diary: Journey of an Irish Coffin Ship.* Cork, Ireland: Mercier Press, 1994.

Woodham-Smith. *The Great Hunger.*

CHAPTER NINE

Arnett, Chris. *The Terror of the Coast.* Burnaby, B.C.: Talonbooks, 1999.

Rolleston, T. W. *High Deeds of Finn: And Other Bardic Romances of Ancient Ireland.* London: G. G. Harrap, 1910.

——. *Myths and Legends of the Celtic Race.*

Sjoestedt, Marie-Louise. *Gods and Heroes of the Celts.* Translated by Myles Dillon. London: Methuen and Co., 1949.

CHAPTER TEN

Armstrong, Karen. *A History of God.* New York: Alfred A. Knopf, 1994.

Davies. *Celtic Spirituality.*

Sharkey, John. *Celtic Mysteries: The Ancient Religion.* New York: Crossroads, 1975.

CHAPTER ELEVEN

Duquette, Joe. *Oral History Film Project Collection.*

Eddy, John A. "Medicine Wheels and Plains Indian Astronomy." In *Astronomy of the Ancients,* edited by Kenneth Brecher and Michael Feirtag. Cambridge, Mass.: The MIT Press, 1979.

Gill, Sam D. *Native American Religions.* Belmont, Ca.: Wadsworth Publishing Co., 1982.

Johnston, Charles M. *The Valley of the Six Nations: A Collection of Documents on the Indian Lands of the Grand River.* Toronto: The Champlain Society, 1964.

Lundy, Randy. "deer-sleep." In *Under the Night Sun.* Regina: Coteau Books, 1999.

Rogers, Edward S., and Donald B. Smith. *Aboriginal Ontario: Historical Perspectives on the First Nations.* Toronto: Dundurn Press, 1994.

Rolleston. *Myths and Legends of the Celtic Race.*

Roy, James Charles. *The Road Wet, the Wind Close: Celtic Ireland.* Dublin: Gill and Macmillan, 1986.

Schmalz, Peter. *The Ojibwa of Southern Ontario.* Toronto: University of Toronto Press, 1991.

Wolfleg, Mark, Sr. *Oral History Film Project Collection.*

CHAPTER TWELVE

Atwood, Margaret. "Further Arrivals." In *Selected Poems, 1966–1984.* Toronto: Oxford University Press, 1990.

Stewart, Frances. *Our Forest Home: Being Extracts from the Correspondence of the Late Frances Stewart.* Edited by E. S. Dunlop. Toronto: Presbyterian Printing and Publishing, 1889. (Made available online by Early Canadiana Online: www.canadiana.org/eco.)

ACKNOWLEDGEMENTS

I AM GRATEFUL TO MANY PEOPLE for the support and help they've given me in the writing of this book. First of all, I want to thank my father, who never stops reminding me about what I want to be doing. My uncle, Jack Smith, who died before this book was published, generously shared his stories with me. My siblings, Anne Pudlo, Mary Greenslade, Pat Hanbury, Barbara Messamore, and Neil Greenslade, offered constant love and support. Special thanks to Barbie for answering my steady stream of history questions. (Any inaccuracies are because I forgot to ask her!) Also special thanks to Neil and his wife, Kate McGinn, for being my first family readers. Thanks to my uncle, Neil Smith, and my aunt, Sylvia Smith, for their kindness and stories, and to my cousins for their hospitality.

I am grateful to Mary Uslick for her patience and generosity in sharing her knowledge. Early suggestions and encouragement came from Barbara Johnston and Jay Draper. To Laura Burkhart and Gerry "The Hyphenator" Hill, thanks for the Saturday nights. I want to thank my students at Saskatchewan Indian Federated College for sharing their stories with me, and for listening to mine. Thanks to Lisa Comeau and Heather Hodgson for insights and reading suggestions, and to Gail Bowen for sharing her wealth of experience. Randy Lundy and Diane Zoell helped take my mind off my deadlines. Keith Maillard set an example as a writer that I have tried to follow; I also want to thank him for his support.

The Canada Council and the Saskatchewan Arts Board gave me financial assistance to write a first draft. Thanks to the Saskatchewan Writers Guild and the Benedictine monks at St. Peter's Abbey for peace and quiet.

My agent Denise Bukowski's belief in the early manuscript gave me the confidence to complete it. Big thanks go to Barbara Berson, my editor at Penguin, for her sensitivity, sense of humour, and an insight that really helped shape this book. Finally, I am grateful to my husband, David Joyce, for his unwavering honesty, for his understanding, and for being beside me not only at every step of the writing of this book, but also during the living of it. Thank you, David, and my sweet son, Khal, for the love that keeps me steady.